REVISE AQA GCSE (9–1) Combined Science: Trilogy
MODEL ANSWER WORKBOOK

Higher

Series Consultant: Harry Smith

Authors: Anne Pilling, Lyn Nicholls and Jen Randall

Also available to support your revision:

Revise GCSE Study Skills Guide 9781447967071

The **Revise GCSE Study Skills Guide** is full of tried-and-trusted hints and tips for how to learn more effectively. It gives you techniques to help you achieve your best – throughout your GCSE studies and beyond!

Revise GCSE Revision Planner 9781447967828

The **Revise GCSE Revision Planner** helps you to plan and organise your time, step-by-step, throughout your GCSE revision. Use this book and wall chart to mastermind your revision.

> For the full range of Pearson revision titles across KS2, KS3, GCSE, Functional Skills, AS/A Level and BTEC visit:
> www.pearsonschools.co.uk/revise

Contents

1 About your exam
2 Command words and mark schemes
3 How to use this book

Biology
4   Cell biology
7   Organisation
10 Infection and response
13 Bioenergetics
17 Homeostasis and response
21 Inheritance, variation and evolution
24 Ecology

Chemistry
28 Atomic structure and the periodic table
31 Bonding, structure, and the properties of matter
33 Quantitative chemistry
35 Chemical changes
38 Energy changes
40 The rate and extent of chemical change
42 Organic chemistry
44 Chemical analysis
47 Chemistry of the atmosphere
50 Using resources

Physics
52 Energy
56 Electricity
60 Particle model of matter
64 Atomic structure
67 Forces
70 Waves
73 Magnetism and electromagnetism

76 Answers

A small bit of small print:
AQA publishes Sample Assessment Material and the Specification on its website. This is the official content and this book should be used in conjunction with it. The questions have been written to help you practise every topic in the book. Remember: the real exam questions may not look like this.

About your exam

Your AQA (9–1) Combined Science: Trilogy GCSE comprises **six exam papers**.

AQA (9–1) Combined Science: Trilogy GCSE is a **double award** exam, which means you will be awarded **two GCSEs**.

Paper 1
Biology
- Cell biology
- Organisation
- Infection and response
- Bioenergetics

Paper 2
Biology
- Homeostasis and response
- Inheritance, variation and evolution
- Ecology

Paper 3
Chemistry
- Atomic structure and the periodic table
- Bonding, structure, and the properties of matter
- Quantitative chemistry
- Chemical changes
- Energy changes

Paper 4
Chemistry
- The rate and extent of chemical change
- Organic chemistry
- Chemical analysis
- Chemistry of the atmosphere
- Using resources

Paper 5
Physics
- Energy
- Electricity
- Particle model of matter
- Atomic structure

Paper 6
Physics
- Forces
- Waves
- Magnetism and electromagnetism

Each paper is...

 written   1 hour 15 minutes   worth 70 marks   16.7% of the total

and will assess your skills and knowledge using a range of question types...

'closed' questions
- multiple-choice
- complete the sentences
- linking the boxes
- label the diagram.

'open' questions
- label/draw the diagram
- write a short response
- write an extended response
- calculate the answer.

AQA (9–1) Combined Science: Trilogy GCSE has two **tiers**: Foundation and Higher. This book is for students planning to sit Higher-tier exams.

Grades available at Higher tier:

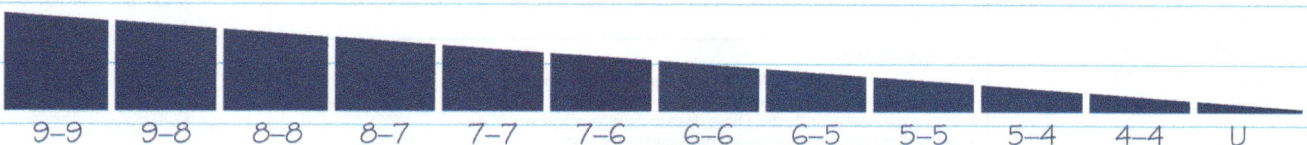

9–9   9–8   8–8   8–7   7–7   7–6   6–6   6–5   5–5   5–4   4–4   U

1

Command words and mark schemes

Understanding command words

A command word tells you how you should answer a question. For some command words, such as **draw**, **complete**, **sketch** and **plot**, it will be clear what you need to do. Some of them, however, are less straightforward. Here is an introduction to some of the more difficult command words and some tips on how to answer questions that use them.

Predict
Suggest the outcome or result of something. Your suggestion must be realistic.

Design/plan
Set out a scientific process or method.

Determine
Use the information given to you to find an answer.

Identify
Recognise or name something.

Evaluate
Gather together all of the data provided and your own knowledge to weigh up evidence for and against something.

Define
Just like a dictionary definition, you need to explain what something means.

Give/name/write
Give a short answer, often just a single word, phrase or sentence. Don't stray into explaining your answer.

Justify
Support a viewpoint using the data provided.

Describe
Give an accurate explanation of what something is, how something works or what happened in a process.

Compare
Write about the similarities and/or differences between things. If you write about just one of the things, you won't be able to get full marks.

Explain
Expand on a statement made in a question. This could involve, for example, giving details about a process or setting out the reasons why something happens.

Suggest
Apply your existing knowledge to a new situation in order to explain how or why something happens.

Understanding mark schemes

Mark schemes tell you what the marker is looking for in your answer. Throughout this book, you will be introduced to using mark schemes alongside exam-style answers. Here are some of the things to look out for.

Closed or short answer mark schemes

Your answer doesn't need to match these points word-for-word, but needs to have the same message and use the correct vocabulary.

Question	Answer	Mark
04.4	idea of placing quadrat randomly	1
	use a sufficient number of quadrat readings	1
	count the number of dandelions growing inside quadrat	1
	estimate dandelion population using: (mean number of dandelions × area of field) ÷ area of quadrat	1

Each mark aligns with a part of the answer, meaning each point is worth one mark.

Extended answer mark schemes

Extended answers are given a level first. Then to award a mark, you need to decide whether the answer is at the top or bottom end of that level.

Level	Answer	Mark
3	A clear, logical explanation is given containing accurate ideas presented in the correct order with links between ideas.	5–6
2	Key ideas are presented with some linked together to form a partial explanation.	3–4
1	Fragmented ideas are given. Some may be relevant with insufficient links to form an explanation.	1–2
	No relevant content	0
	Indicative content • dead or weakened form of the bacteria used to create a vaccine • vaccine causes immune system to react • the dead / weakened bacteria have disease-causing antigens • white blood cells/lymphocytes are produced by the body • they make specific antibodies for the antigen which destroy the antigens • memory cells remain in the body • if the same antigen returns the body can produce antibodies very quickly	

The indicative content section is a guide to the sorts of points that would be included in a good answer. The list is not 'exhaustive', which means there may be other correct answers.

How to use this book

In this book, you will familiarise yourself with the AQA (9–1) Combined Science: Trilogy GCSE by engaging with exam-style questions, answers and mark schemes. Doing so means you will know exactly what to expect in the exam and, just as importantly, what will be expected of you in the exam.

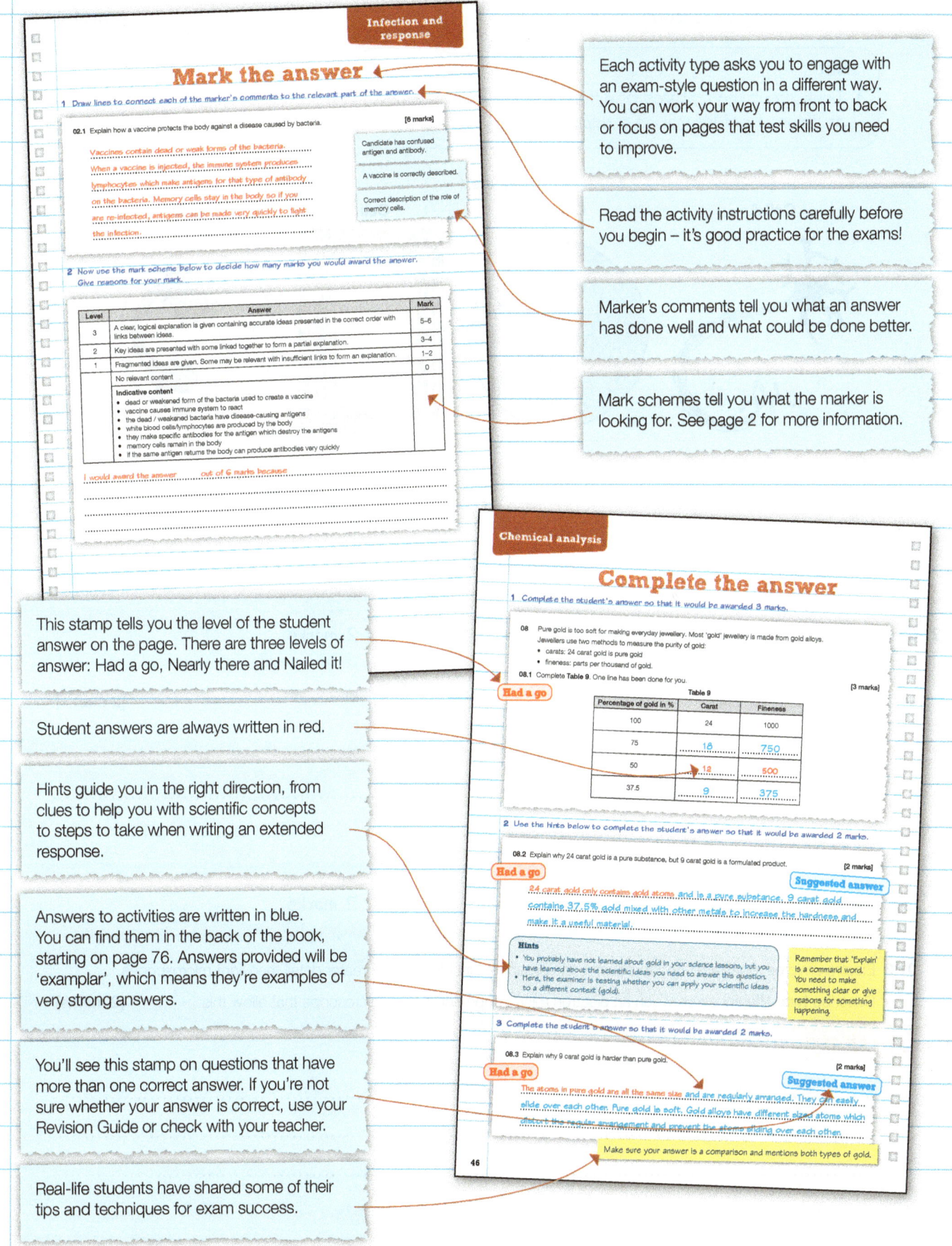

Each activity type asks you to engage with an exam-style question in a different way. You can work your way from front to back or focus on pages that test skills you need to improve.

Read the activity instructions carefully before you begin – it's good practice for the exams!

Marker's comments tell you what an answer has done well and what could be done better.

Mark schemes tell you what the marker is looking for. See page 2 for more information.

This stamp tells you the level of the student answer on the page. There are three levels of answer: Had a go, Nearly there and Nailed it!

Student answers are always written in red.

Hints guide you in the right direction, from clues to help you with scientific concepts to steps to take when writing an extended response.

Answers to activities are written in blue. You can find them in the back of the book, starting on page 76. Answers provided will be 'exemplar', which means they're examples of very strong answers.

You'll see this stamp on questions that have more than one correct answer. If you're not sure whether your answer is correct, use your Revision Guide or check with your teacher.

Real-life students have shared some of their tips and techniques for exam success.

3

Cell biology

Complete the answer

1 Use the hint below to complete the student's answer so that it would be awarded 2 marks.

03.1 Which of the cells shown in **Figure 1** is **not** an animal cell?

Give **one** reason for your answer. [2 marks]

> **Hint**
> - Think about the features of different cells. Look carefully at Figure 1 before making a decision.

Figure 1

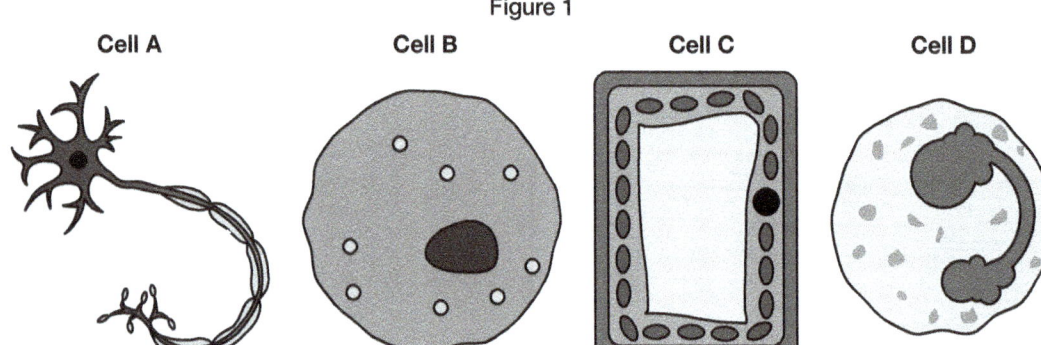

Cell A   Cell B   Cell C   Cell D

Nearly there

Cell: *C* ....

Reason: ....

---

2 Complete the student's answer so that it would be awarded 2 marks.

06.2 Why are stem cells used in medicine? [2 marks]

Had a go

Stem cells have not differentiated ....

....

---

3 Complete the student's answer so that it would be awarded 2 marks.

01.2 Electron microscopes are used to observe the organelles inside cells in greater detail than light microscopes.

Describe **two** differences between an electron microscope and a light microscope that allow this. [2 marks]

Nearly there

An electron microscope has a much higher magnification ....

....

....

4

Cell biology

Complete the question

1 Complete the question by adding **two** multiple-choice options. Make sure one is correct.

03.1 Each statement below gives two structures found in cells.

Which statement gives structures that are found in **both** prokaryotic and eukaryotic cells?

Tick **one** box. [1 mark]

Mitochondria and nucleus ☐

.... ✓

.... ☐

Cytoplasm and nucleus ☐

---

2 Complete the question by adding **two** multiple-choice options. Make sure one is correct.

04.2 Which of the following diseases can be treated using stem cells?

Tick **one** box. [1 mark]

.... ☐

.... ✓

Obesity ☐

High blood pressure ☐

> Multiple-choice answers always contain believable answers. Make sure your incorrect options really test the understanding of the question.

3 Use the answer below to complete the question.

02.1 The image of a cell in a textbook is .... in length.

The real cell is only ....

Calculate the magnification of the cell. [4 marks]

Magnification = size of image ÷ size of real object

5.2 cm = 52 mm

52 mm = 52 000 μm

Magnification = 52 000 ÷ 130 μm

Magnification of the cell = × 400

Cell biology

Mark the answer

1. Use the mark scheme below to decide how many marks you would award the answer. Give reasons for your mark.

05.1 Active transport allows mineral ions to be absorbed into plant roots.

Explain how mineral ions are absorbed from the soil. **[6 marks]**

Active transport moves substances against a concentration gradient from a low concentration to a higher concentration using energy from respiration.

> There are some key ideas stated. The ideas given are linked together in a logical way to give a partial explanation.

Level	Answer	Mark
3	A clear, logical explanation is provided containing accurate ideas presented in the correct order with links between ideas.	5–6
2	Key ideas of the context are presented with some ideas linked together to form a partial explanation.	3–4
1	Fragmented ideas are described. Some may be relevant with insufficient links to form an explanation. The response may explain active transport but not link it to the context.	1–2
	No relevant content	0
	Indicative content • active transport occurs when mineral ions are being moved from a low concentration to a high concentration • the concentration of mineral ions is higher inside the root hair cell than in the soil • mineral ions need to be taken into the cell against the concentration gradient • carrier molecules are used to transport mineral ions across the cell membrane • energy is required to make the carrier molecules work • carrier molecules are specific for each substance • the energy comes from respiration • mineral ions are then released into the root hair cell • this increases the concentration inside the cell	

I would award the answer .... out of 6 marks because ....

Organisation

Improve the answer

1 Use the hint below to write an improved answer that would be awarded 3 marks.

> 03.1 Different enzymes catalyse different reactions.
>
> Explain why enzymes are specific and only catalyse one reaction. **[3 marks]**
>
> **Had a go**
>
> It is like a key in a lock.
>
> **Hint**
> - This answer doesn't go far enough in its explanation. What is like a key in a lock and how is it like a key in a lock?
>
> ....
>
> ....
>
> ....

2 Use the hints below to write an improved answer that would be awarded 6 marks.

> 04.3 In plant leaves, there are different tissues that have different functions.
>
> Explain how the structure of the tissues in a leaf is related to their functions. **[6 marks]**
>
> **Had a go**
>
> Some have no chloroplasts to let the light pass through. Some have lots of chloroplasts. Others are like tubes that carry water and sugar. Stomata open and close to let water out and allow carbon dioxide in.
>
> **Hints**
> - This answer has identified some of the ways that tissues are differentiated but there isn't much explanation.
> - This answer also uses very few scientific names for plant tissues or processes.
> - Make sure you match each plant tissue with the correct function.
> - You need to give a detailed description of most of the structures **and** their functions.
>
> ....
>
> ....
>
> ....
>
> ....
>
> ....
>
> ....

Organisation

Find the answer

1 Use the mark scheme to find the answer that would be awarded 2 marks. Choose **A, B** or **C**. Explain your choice.

05.1 Doctors calculate the waist-to-hip ratio of a patient to decide if the patient is at risk of developing cardiovascular disease.

Calculate the waist-to-hip ratio for someone with a waist measurement of 0.66 m and a hip measurement of 96 cm.

Give your answer to two significant figures. [2 marks]

Question	Answer	Extra information	Mark
05.1	96 cm = 0.96 m 0.66 ÷ 0.96 **or** 0.66 m = 66 cm 66 ÷ 96 = 0.6875 = 0.69	allow 0.69 with no working shown for **2** marks	1 1

A Ratio = 0.66 ÷ 0.96 = 0.6875 = 0.69

B Ratio = 0.66 ÷ 96 = 0.006875 = 0.0069

C Ratio = 0.688

Answer .... would be awarded 2 marks because ....

....

2 Use the mark scheme to find the answer that would be awarded 2 marks. Choose **A, B** or **C**. Explain your choice.

06.5 Give **two** risk factors for cardiovascular disease. [2 marks]

Question	Answer	Mark
06.5	any **two** from: • poor diet • smoking • lack of exercise	2

A Eating too much fat and sugar, and smoking

B Smoking and other unhealthy lifestyle choices

C Too much TV and not exercising

Answer .... would be awarded 2 marks because ....

....

Mark the answer

Organisation

1 Use the mark scheme below to decide how many marks you would award the answer. Give reasons for your mark.

07 A student investigated how air movement affects transpiration. The student set up two potometers as shown in **Figure 2**.

Figure 2

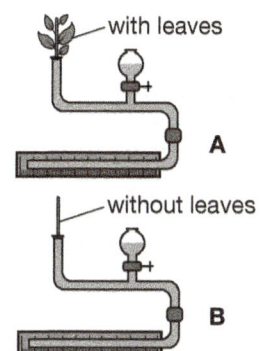

with leaves

A

without leaves

B

07.1 Describe what will happen.

Explain the results. [6 marks]

In A, the meniscus will move to the right more than in B because of transpiration, where water is lost from the leaves by evaporation and diffusion. More air movement means more transpiration because the concentration gradient is increased.

Level	Answer	Mark
3	A clear, logical explanation containing a description of water movement in both potometers is provided and a detailed explanation of how the fan causes loss of water to increase due to increased diffusion / evaporation because of lower humidity outside the leaf / increased diffusion gradient is given.	5–6
2	Key ideas are presented with some linked together. There may be a description of water movement in both potometers and a simple explanation that the fan causes loss of water to increase.	3–4
1	Fragmented answer given with a description of water movement in both potometers or a simple explanation that the fan causes loss of water.	1–2
	No relevant content	0
	Indicative content **description**: • water meniscus moves to the right in A but does not move in B **explanation**: • air movement / the fan causes greater loss of water from the potometer • because water is lost from the leaves by evaporation (or diffusion) of water • air movement / the fan lowers the concentration of water / humidity outside the plant • air movement / the fan increases (or maintains) the concentration gradient • air movement / fan increases (or maintains) the diffusion gradient	

I would award the answer   out of 6 marks because

Infection and response

Complete the answer

1 Complete the student's answer so that it would be awarded 2 marks.

> **08.3** Describe how mosquitoes spread malaria. [2 marks]
>
> **Had a go**
>
> Mosquitoes suck infected blood ....

2 Complete the student's answer so that it would be awarded 2 marks.

> **04.1** The plant disease rose black spot is caused by a fungus.
>
> Describe the symptoms of rose black spot and the possible treatments. [2 marks]
>
> **Had a go**
>
> The symptoms are purple or black spots on the leaves and stem. ....

3 Complete the student's answer so that it would be awarded 2 marks.

> **05** Table 1 shows the number of people infected with an antibiotic-resistant strain of bacteria.
>
> Table 1
>
> | Year | 2008 | 2009 | 2010 | 2011 |
> |---|---|---|---|---|
> | Number of people infected with the antibiotic-resistant strain of bacteria | 2067 | 2143 | 2314 | 2576 |
>
> **05.1** Calculate the percentage increase in the number of people infected between 2008 and 2011.
>
> Give your answer to two significant figures. [2 marks]
>
> **Nearly there**
>
> $$\frac{\text{Number in 2011} - \text{number in 2008}}{\text{number in 2008}} \times 100$$
>
> Percentage increase = ... %

> Although the correct answer with no working out would be awarded 2 marks, it is always better to show your working out.

10

Mark the answer

Infection and response

1 Draw lines to connect each of the marker's comments to the relevant part of the answer.

02.1 Explain how a vaccine protects the body against a disease caused by bacteria. **[6 marks]**

Vaccines contain dead or weak forms of the bacteria. When a vaccine is injected, the immune system produces lymphocytes which make antigens for that type of antibody on the bacteria. Memory cells stay in the body so if you are re-infected, antigens can be made very quickly to fight the infection.

- Candidate has confused antigen and antibody.
- A vaccine is correctly described.
- Correct description of the role of memory cells.

---

2 Now use the mark scheme below to decide how many marks you would award the answer. Give reasons for your mark.

Level	Answer	Mark
3	A clear, logical explanation is given containing accurate ideas presented in the correct order with links between ideas.	5–6
2	Key ideas are presented with some linked together to form a partial explanation.	3–4
1	Fragmented ideas are given. Some may be relevant with insufficient links to form an explanation.	1–2
	No relevant content	0
	Indicative content • dead or weakened form of the bacteria used to create a vaccine • vaccine causes immune system to react • the dead / weakened bacteria have disease-causing antigens • white blood cells/lymphocytes are produced by the body • they make specific antibodies for the antigen which destroy the antigens • memory cells remain in the body • if the same antigen returns the body can produce antibodies very quickly	

I would award the answer .... out of 6 marks because ....

....

....

....

11

Infection and response

Complete the question

1 Complete the question by adding **two** multiple-choice options. Make sure one is correct.

> 05.2 Which of these statements gives **two** diseases caused by bacterial infections?
>
> Tick **one** box. [1 mark]
>
> Measles and salmonella ☐
>
> Malaria and measles ☐
>
> .... ✓
>
> .... ☐

2 Use the hints and answer below to complete the question.

> 06.1 Explain ....
>
> Tick **one** box. [1 mark]
>
> **Hints**
> - Use the correct answers to work out what concept is being explained.
> - The incorrect answers might help you eliminate some options.
>
> **Nailed it!**
>
> A trial where the patient does not know if they are taking a drug or a placebo. ☐
>
> A trial where the doctor does not know if the patient is taking a drug or a placebo. ☐
>
> A trial where the patient and doctor do not know if the patient is taking a drug or a placebo. ✓
>
> A trial where the doctor and the pharmaceutical company making the drug do not know if the patient is taking the drug or a placebo. ☐

Bioenergetics

Find the answer

1 Use the mark scheme to find the answer that would be awarded 2 marks. Choose **A, B, C or D**. Explain your choice.

03.1 What is the symbol equation for photosynthesis? [2 marks]

Question	Answer	Mark
03.1	correct reactants $CO_2 + H_2O$	1
	correct products $C_6H_{12}O_6 + O_2$	1

A $CO_2 + H_2O \rightarrow C_6H_{12}O_6 + CO_2$

B   water $+ CO_2 \rightarrow O_2 +$ energy $+ C_6H_{12}O_6$

C $O_2 + H_2O \rightarrow C_6H_{12}O_6 + O_2$

D $CO_2 + H_2O \rightarrow C_6H_{12}O_6 + O_2$

Answer .... would be awarded 2 marks because ....

....

2 Use the mark scheme to find the answer that would be awarded 1 mark. Choose **A, B or C**. Explain your choice.

04.2 Why is less energy transferred during anaerobic respiration than aerobic respiration? [1 mark]

Question	Answer	Mark
04.2	oxidation of glucose is incomplete in anaerobic respiration	1

A   Aerobic respiration produces much more energy than anaerobic respiration because the oxidation of glucose is incomplete in anaerobic respiration.

B   Aerobic respiration produces much more energy than anaerobic respiration because the oxidation of glucose is complete in anaerobic respiration.

C   Aerobic respiration produces much more energy than anaerobic respiration because the oxidation of glucose is incomplete.

Answer .... would be awarded 1 mark because ....

....

....

....

Bioenergetics

Complete the question

1 Complete the question by adding **two** multiple-choice options. Make sure one is correct.

> **03.3** Which of the following is the correct word equation for anaerobic respiration in yeast cells?
>
> Tick **one** box. [1 mark]
>
> glucose + oxygen → lactic acid + carbon dioxide ☐
>
> glucose → lactic acid ☐
>
> .... ✓
>
> .... ☐

2 Use the answer below to complete the question.

> **04** A student investigated the effect of light intensity on photosynthesis.
>
> Her results are shown in **Figure 3**.
>
>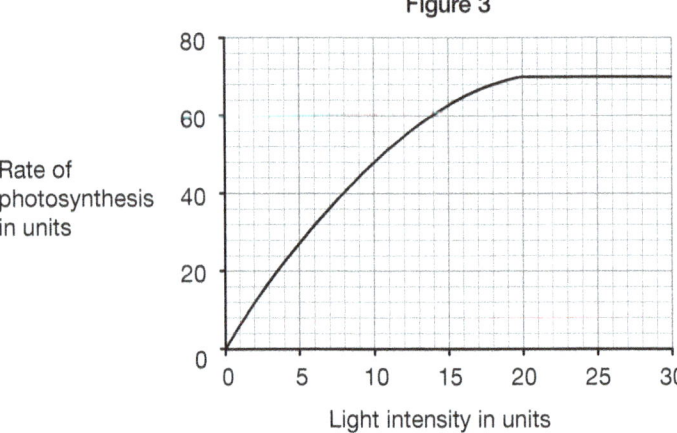
>
> **04.1** Name **two** factors that ....
>
> Tick **one** box. [1 mark]
>
> **Nailed it!**
>
> Amount of chlorophyll and minerals ☐
>
> Temperature and amount of light ☐
>
> Amount of chlorophyll and temperature ✓
>
> Amount of carbon dioxide and light ☐

Bioenergetics

Re-order the answer

1 Rearrange the statements into the most logical order by numbering each part of the answer.

05.4 Describe the method used to investigate the effect of light intensity on the rate of photosynthesis. **[4 marks]**

☐ Place the beaker containing the pondweed 10cm away from a light source.

☐ Repeat the investigation with the beaker containing the pondweed 20cm, 30cm and 40cm away from the light source.

☐ Take some pondweed and place it in a beaker of water in the light. Check that the pondweed is photosynthesising by looking for bubbles of oxygen being released.

☐ Leave the pondweed for 5 minutes. Then use a stopwatch to count the number of bubbles produced in 1 minute by the pondweed.

When you are asked a question about a required practical, try to remember what you did when you carried out the investigation.

2 Rearrange the sentences into the most logical order by numbering each part of the answer.

06 A student is investigating the relationship between light intensity and photosynthesis.

The student measures the rate of photosynthesis for pondweed in a test tube at different distances from a light source. Light intensity is inversely proportional to the square of the distance (d) from the light source.

Light intensity = $1 \div d^2$

06.1 Suggest how the student could analyse the relationship between light intensity and the rate of photosynthesis.

Use the equation in your answer. **[4 marks]**

☐ Square the distance between the lamp and the plant.

☐ Plot a graph of the rate of photosynthesis against $1 \div d^2$.

☐ The graph should show that the rate of photosynthesis increases with light intensity.

☐ Calculate the inverse of the distance from the lamp to the plant.

Bioenergetics

Improve the answer

1 Use the hint below to write an improved answer that would be awarded 4 marks.

07.1 Pine trees often grow on exposed hillsides.

The cooler temperatures, windy conditions and dry soil affect the growth of the trees.

How would this affect the growth of trees? Explain why. [4 marks]

Had a go

Lower temperatures and high winds decrease the rate of photosynthesis.

Hint
- The student has correctly identified the factors affecting growth but hasn't explained how and why these factors have affected it.

2 Write an improved answer that would be awarded 4 marks.

08.1 The apparatus shown in **Figure 4** can be used to measure respiration in peas.

Describe the results you would expect. Explain why. [4 marks]

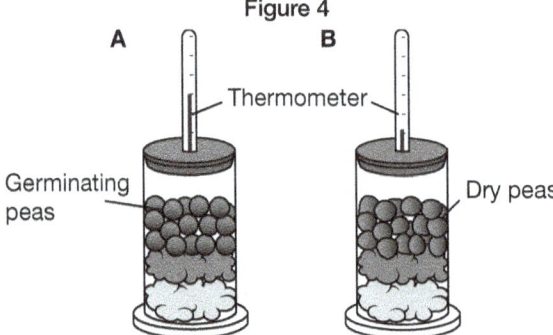

Figure 4

Had a go

Flask A contains germinating peas that are respiring and Flask B contains peas that are not respiring.

16

Homeostasis and response

Mark the answer

1 Draw lines to connect each of the marker's comments to the relevant part of the answer.

01.4 Explain how glucagon interacts with insulin to control blood sugar. **[6 marks]**

Insulin and glucagon balance blood sugar levels using negative feedback. When blood glucose is too high after a meal, insulin in the blood makes the liver convert glucose to glycogen to store it and lower the blood sugar level. If blood sugar is too low, insulin production stops and glucagon in the blood makes the liver change the glycogen into glucose to increase blood glucose. No more glucagon is then produced.

- Correct description of the role of the liver.
- No mention of the role of the pancreas in monitoring blood glucose and secreting insulin.
- The explanation is constructed well in a step-by-step way. It follows the negative feedback cycle clearly, starting with what happens when blood sugar is too high and then explaining what happens when blood sugar levels are too low.

---

2 Now use the mark scheme below to decide how many marks you would award the answer. Give reasons for your mark.

Level	Answer	Mark
3	A clear, logical explanation is given containing accurate ideas presented in the correct order with links made between ideas.	5–6
2	Key ideas are presented with some linked together to form a partial explanation.	3–4
1	Fragmented ideas are presented. Some may be relevant, with insufficient links to form an explanation.	1–2
	No relevant content.	0
	Indicative content • cells in pancreas detect/monitor blood glucose concentration • if blood glucose concentration is too high, the pancreas secretes insulin into blood • at the liver/target organ, blood glucose is absorbed and converted into glycogen for storage • if blood glucose level is too low, pancreas secretes glucagon into blood • at the liver/target organ, glycogen is converted into glucose and released into the blood • this is a negative feedback cycle	

I would award the answer   out of 6 marks because

Homeostasis and response

Complete the answer

1 Complete the student's answer so that it would be awarded 2 marks.

> **11.2** There are two types of diabetes.
>
> Explain how Type 1 diabetes differs from Type 2 diabetes. **[2 marks]**
>
> Type 1 diabetes happens due to ....
>
> ....
>
> It can be treated by insulin injections. Type 2 diabetes happens due to ....
>
> ....
>
> It can be treated by ....
>
> ....

2 Complete the student's answer so that it would be awarded 3 marks.

> **07.2** Explain how the endocrine system works to control and co-ordinate the body. **[3 marks]**
>
> The endocrine system consists of ....
>
> ....
>
> Hormones are secreted ....
>
> ....
>
> Hormones work on ....
>
> ....

3 Complete the student's answer so that it would be awarded 4 marks.

> **04.3** In vitro fertilisation (IVF) is used to treat infertility.
>
> Explain the advantages and disadvantages of IVF. **[4 marks]**
>
> The benefit of using IVF is that it ....
>
> ....
>
> However, the disadvantages of using IVF are ....
>
> ....
>
> ....
>
> This is ....
>
> ....

Homeostasis and response

Complete the question

1 Complete the question by adding **two** multiple-choice options. Make sure one is correct.

06.2 Why is homeostasis important in living things?

Tick **one** box. [1 mark]

.... ☑

.... ☐

It ensures that cells have sufficient oxygen for respiration. ☐

It makes sure that reaction times in animals are very fast. ☐

---

2 Use the answer below to complete the question.

05.3 Negative feedback systems control hormone levels in the blood.

Explain .... [2 marks]

Nailed it!

> The hypothalmus detects a drop in internal body temperature and low levels of thyroxine in the blood. This triggers the hypothalmus to send a message to the pituitary gland to release TSH. Increased levels of TSH cause the thyroid gland to produce thyroxine. Thyroxine increases metabolic rate. When higher thyroxine levels are detected by the hypothalmus and pituitary gland, they inhibit the release of TSH and thyroxine levels in the blood drop.

---

3 Use the multiple-choice options below to complete the question.

03.2 Which .... [1 mark]

Nailed it!

Oestrogen and follicle-stimulating hormone ☐

Oestrogen and luteinising hormone ☐

Luteinising hormone and progesterone ☐

Follicle-stimulating hormone and luteinising hormone ☑

Homeostasis and response

Re-order the answer

1 Rearrange the sentences into the most logical order by numbering each part of the answer.

06.3 Explain how hormones are used to treat infertility. [4 marks]

- [ ] The eggs are removed from the mother and fertilised by sperm from the father in the laboratory.
- [ ] When the embryos are tiny balls of cells, they are inserted into the uterus of the mother.
- [ ] The eggs develop into embryos in the laboratory.
- [ ] The mother takes FSH and LH to stimulate the maturation of some eggs.

> Once you have decided on the order of the statements, read them through in that order to ensure that the answer makes sense.

2 Rearrange the sentences into the most logical order by numbering each part of the answer.

07.5 Describe an investigation into reaction times using the ruler drop test. [4 marks]

- [ ] Student B drops the ruler without telling Student A; Student A must catch the ruler as quickly as possible.
- [ ] Student B holds a ruler vertically above Student A's hand.
- [ ] The number level with the top of Student A's thumb is recorded and the test is repeated ten times.
- [ ] Student A places their arm across a table with their hand hanging over the edge.

> When you are answering a question about a required practical, think about when you carried out the activity in the lab.

Inheritance, variation and evolution

Complete the answer

1 Complete the student's answer so that it would be awarded 4 marks.

> **02.1** Cystic fibrosis is caused by a recessive allele (f). A mother has cystic fibrosis, and the father is heterozygous for the condition. What is the probability that their baby has cystic fibrosis too?
>
> Draw a genetic diagram to explain your answer. **[4 marks]**
>
> **Had a go**
>
> The mother has cystic fibrosis, which is caused by a recessive allele, so she must have the ff genotype.

2 Complete the student's answer so that it would be awarded 3 marks.

> **12.4** Explain how evolution occurs through natural selection. **[3 marks]**
>
> **Had a go**
>
> There is variation between organisms of the same species.

3 Complete the student's answer so that it would be awarded 2 marks.

> **04.7** Complete the sentences to explain how a new species is formed.
> Use words from the box. **[2 marks]**
>
> **Nearly there**
>
> | phenotype | ~~breed~~ | genotype | environment |
>
> A species is a group of similar organisms which are able to ......**breed**...... together to produce fertile offspring. A new species is formed when two populations of the same species become so different in .... that they can no longer interbreed.

21

Inheritance, variation and evolution

Complete the question

1 Use the hints and the answer below to complete the question.

03.1 Farmers use selective breeding to produce animals that will increase food production.

Describe .... [2 marks]

Nailed it!

If one animal catches a disease, they will all get it as all the animals will be susceptible to the same disease. It may also lead to more inherited defects because of inbreeding.

Hints
- Think about susceptibility to disease.
- Think about problems associated with inbreeding.

2 Complete the question by adding **two** multiple-choice options. Make sure one is correct.

02.1 Polydactyly causes extra fingers and toes.

The condition is controlled by a dominant allele (P).

The mother is heterozygous and the father is homozygous recessive for the condition.

What is the probability of their child having polydactyly?

Tick **one** box. [1 mark]

0.25 ☐

.... ✓

.... ☐

1 ☐

Re-order the answer

1 Rearrange the sentences into the most logical order by numbering each part of the answer.

02.2 Explain how bacteria are genetically modified to produce human insulin. [5 marks]

- [ ] Insert the insulin gene into the plasmid.
- [ ] Remove and process the human insulin produced.
- [ ] Use an enzyme to remove the gene that codes for insulin production from the chromosome of a pancreas cell.
- [ ] Return the plasmid to the bacterial cell and culture the bacteria.
- [ ] Use an enzyme to remove a plasmid from a bacterial cell and to cut it.

2 Rearrange the sentences into the most logical order by numbering each part of the answer.

07.6 Gametes are sex cells containing genetic information.
Explain how gametes are formed. [4 marks]

- [ ] Similar chromosomes pair up.
- [ ] In the sex organs, chromosomes make identical copies of their DNA.
- [ ] Sections of DNA are exchanged between chromosomes.
- [ ] Pairs of chromosomes divide to form gametes with half the original chromosome number.

Ecology

Complete the question

1 Use the student's answer below to complete the question.

> **12.1** All species live in ecosystems. They consist of communities of plants and animals that are adapted to the abiotic and biotic conditions of that ecosystem.
>
> Name .... [1 mark]
>
> *Nailed it!*
>
> Temperature, light intensity, carbon dioxide levels ....

The answer lists three things so you know that the question must have asked for three factors.

2 Complete the question by adding **two** multiple-choice options. Make sure one is correct.

> **07.1** Which **one** of the following may cause water pollution?
>
> Tick **one** box. [1 mark]
>
> Smoke ☐
>
> Landfill ☐
>
> .... ☑
>
> .... ☐

3 Complete the question by adding **two** multiple-choice options. Make sure one is correct.

> **08.4** Which of the following is a reason for the large-scale deforestation happening in some countries?
>
> Tick **one** box. [1 mark]
>
> .... ☐
>
> For new landfill sites ☐
>
> .... ☑
>
> To provide new habitats to increase biodiversity ☐

24

Re-order the answer

1 Rearrange the sentences into the most logical order by numbering each part of the answer. One has been done for you.

04.4 Describe the main stages of the carbon cycle. [5 marks]

- [4] Animals and plants die and are eaten by decomposers. The carbon in the dead organisms is released back into the atmosphere as carbon dioxide.

- [3] Consumers feed on plants, passing the carbon in them up the food chain.

- [2] Producers use carbon dioxide in the atmosphere to photosynthesise and make carbohydrates.

- [1] When animals and plants respire, and fuels are burned, carbon is released into the atmosphere.

- [5] If dead animals and plants cannot decompose, fossil fuels containing carbon may be formed.

2 Rearrange the sentences into the most logical order by numbering each part of the answer.

05.1 Some animal populations are dependent on each other. Lions are predators that feed on gazelles.

Explain how the lion population affects the gazelle population. [2 marks]

- [2] Lions eat gazelles and the gazelle population falls.

- [1] There is plenty of food for lions to feed and reproduce, so their population increases.

- [3] There is insufficient food to maintain the lion population so the lion population falls.

- [4] Fewer lions are feeding on gazelles, so the gazelle population starts to increase.

25

Ecology

Mark the answer

1 Use the mark scheme below to decide how many marks you would award the answer. Give reasons for your mark.

---

01 Two students investigated the number of woodlice in the school garden. This is the method used.

1. Catch 30–40 woodlice.
2. Mark all of the woodlice, then release them.
3. After 4 days, catch 30–40 woodlice.
4. Count the number of marked woodlice in the second sample.

Table 2 shows the results.

Table 2

Number of woodlice in first sample	Number of woodlice in second sample	Number of marked woodlice in second sample
40	35	7

01.1 Calculate the size of the woodlice population. [2 marks]

Population size = $\dfrac{\text{number in first sample} \times \text{number in second sample}}{\text{number in second sample that were marked}} = \dfrac{40 \times 35}{7}$

= 2000 woodlice

Question	Answer	Mark
01.1	(40 × 35) ÷ 7	1
	= 200	1

I would award the answer .... out of 2 marks because ....

---

2 Use the mark scheme below to decide how many marks you would award the answer. Give reasons for your mark.

04.4 Describe how quadrats should be used to estimate the number of dandelion plants in a field. [4 marks]

Put the quadrat down on the field 10 times and count the dandelions in the quadrat.

Question	Answer	Mark
04.4	idea of placing quadrat randomly	1
	use a sufficient number of quadrat readings	1
	count the number of dandelions growing inside quadrat	1
	estimate dandelion population using: (mean number of dandelions × area of field) ÷ area of quadrat	1

I would award the answer .... out of 4 marks because ....

Ecology

Complete the answer

1 Complete the student's answer so that it would be awarded 2 marks.

> **03.1** Carbon dioxide is a greenhouse gas that causes global warming. 82% of the carbon dioxide released each year comes from combustion. The total amount of carbon dioxide released is 780 million tonnes.
>
> Calculate the mass released by combustion to two significant figures. **[2 marks]**
>
> **Nearly there**
>
> Mass released by combustion = $\dfrac{\text{\% released by combustion}}{100}$ × total mass released
>
> ....
>
> ....
>
> Mass released by combustion = ... million tonnes

2 Complete the student's answer so that it would be awarded 2 marks.

> **02.1** Peat is used by many gardeners to improve the quality of soil.
>
> Explain the impact of the destruction of peat bogs on the environment. **[2 marks]**
>
> The destruction of peat bogs reduces ....
>
> ....
>
> ....

3 Complete the student's answer so that it would be awarded 4 marks.

> **06.2** Describe how quadrats can be used to estimate the number of thistles in a farmer's field. **[4 marks]**
>
> The area of the field and ....
>
> ....
>
> A quadrat is placed ....
>
> ....
>
> This is repeated ....
>
> ....
>
> ....

27

Atomic structure and the periodic table

Re-order the answer

1 Rearrange the sentences into the most logical order by numbering each part of the answer.

01 **Figure 5** shows the apparatus used in an alpha particle scattering experiment.

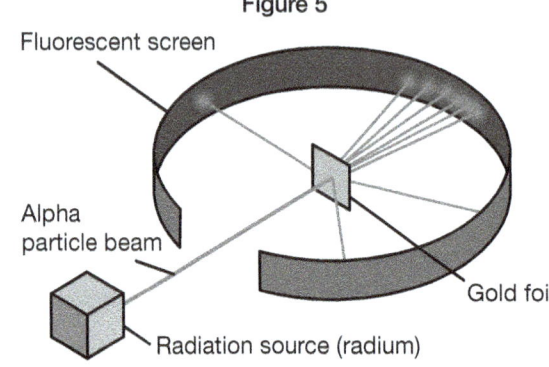

Figure 5

01.1 Explain how the results led to the discovery of charged nuclei in atoms. [3 marks]

Hint
- 'Explain' is the command word here. That means making something clear and saying how it happened.

☐ They also concluded that the central mass of the atom must be charged.

☐ Some particles passed straight through, but a few were deflected and some reflected.

☐ Positively charged alpha particles were fired at gold foil.

☐ Scientists concluded that most of the mass in an atom must be in the centre.

☐ The alpha particles are very small and should have passed straight through the foil.

☐ They called the central mass the nucleus.

Atomic structure and the periodic table

Complete the answer

1 Use the hints below to complete the student's answer so that it would be awarded 3 marks.

05 Naturally occurring chlorine has two isotopes.

Table 3 gives their mass numbers and abundances.

Table 3

Isotope	Abundance of isotope in %
$^{35}_{17}Cl$	75
$^{37}_{17}Cl$	25

05.1 Use the formula below to calculate the relative atomic mass of chlorine. [3 marks]

Relative atomic mass = $\dfrac{(\text{mass} \times \text{abundance of isotope 1}) + (\text{mass} \times \text{abundance of isotope 2})}{100}$

> **Hints**
> - 'Calculate' is a command word. You must use the numbers in the question to work out the answer.
> - Remember to show all your working. You may get some marks, even if you get an incorrect answer.

Relative atomic mass of chlorine = $\dfrac{(35 \times 75) +}{100}$

Relative atomic mass = ...

2 Use the hints below to complete the student's answer so that it would be awarded 2 marks.

03.1 The diameter of one chlorine atom is 0.175 nm or 1.75×10^{-10} m.

The diameter of a chlorine nucleus is 1.00×10^{-14} m.

How many times bigger is the diameter of the chlorine atom than the diameter of its nucleus? [2 marks]

Number of times bigger = $\dfrac{}{1.00 \times 10^{-14}}$

Number of times bigger = ...

> **Hint**
> - Decide whether to use the measurement in nm or m for the diameter of a chlorine atom.

Make sure you know how to do standard form calculations on your calculator. You learned these skills in your Maths lessons.

Atomic structure and the periodic table

Complete the question

1 Use the hint and the answer below to complete the question.

01 These are the electronic structures of atoms of different elements.

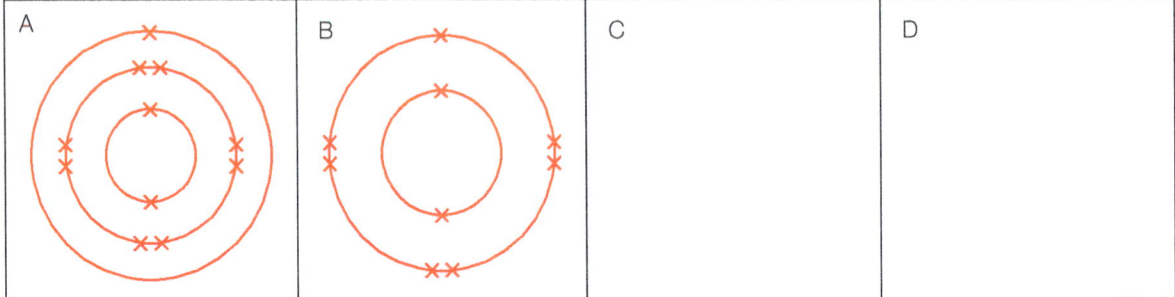

01.1 Which element is very unreactive? [1 mark]

Nailed it!

Element C is very unreactive.

Hint
- There are several possible options in this question. Your correct answer, C, must represent an element that is unreactive because of its electronic structure. Your incorrect answer must represent elements that are reactive because of their electronic structures.

2 Use the answer below to complete the question.

01.2 An atom of element E has an electronic structure of 2,8,5. Its mass number is 31.

How .... [1 mark]

Nailed it!

31 − 15 = 16

> Notice the question numbers. The questions in your GCSE exam will be numbered like this. 01.1 and 01.2 are part of the same question.

Bonding, structure, and the properties of matter

Mark the answer

1 Draw lines to connect each of the marker's comments to the relevant part of the answer.

---

01 **Table 4** shows the melting points of sodium chloride and chlorine.

Table 4

Substance	Melting point in °C
Sodium chloride	801
Chlorine gas	−102

01.1 Explain the difference in melting points of sodium chloride and chlorine gas.

Use ideas about bonding and structure in your answer.

[6 marks]

Sodium chloride has ionic bonding and chlorine has covalent. It takes a lot of energy to melt sodium chloride because the bonds have to be broken. Chlorine also needs a lot of energy to break its bonds, but covalent bonds break more easily. Chlorine is more reactive than sodium chloride because chlorine atoms need another electron.

- This is not asked for in the question.
- It would be clearer to name ionic bonds, but this can be inferred from the previous sentence.
- Type of bonding correctly identified in both substances.
- Covalent bonds are not broken. The answer does not include intermolecular forces.

---

2 Now use the mark scheme below to decide how many marks you would award the answer. Give reasons for your mark.

You can only award marks for relevant information.

Level	Answer	Mark
3	The answer correctly identifies the bonding and type of structure in both substances. The changes that occur when the substances melt are identified. The energy required to break bonds is linked to the bonding and structure. The answer is logical and uses scientific language.	5–6
2	The answer correctly identifies the type of bonding in the substances. Some of the changes at the melting point are identified. An attempt is made to link these changes to the melting and boiling points.	3–4
1	Simple statements are made. There is little explanation of the difference in melting points.	1–2

I would award the answer .... out of 6 marks because ....

....

....

....

....

....

This question continues on page 32.

Bonding, structure, and the properties of matter

Improve the answer

1 On page 31, you used a mark scheme to mark an answer. Use the hints below to write an improved answer that would be awarded 6 marks.

Hints
- Extended answers should have a logical structure.
- Beware of using 'it' or 'they' in answers. It may not be clear what you are referring to and you may lose marks.

> Your GCSE exam papers will have questions that continue over several pages. You may need to refer back to previous pages for information. Always check the numbering of the questions.

....
....
....
....
....
....
....

2 Use the marker's comments to write an improved answer that would be awarded 3 marks.

01.2 The particle theory can be used to describe sodium chloride and chlorine melting. It does not explain why sodium chloride and chlorine have different melting points.

Give **three** limitations of the particle theory when describing sodium chloride and chlorine melting. **[3 marks]**

Had a go

Limitation 1: *They are all the same size.*

It is not clear what 'They' refers to. Answer needs to be more specific.

....
....
....

Limitation 2: *Sodium chloride particles are strongly attracted to each other.*

The student recognises attractions exist between particles but has not applied this to the particle theory.

....
....
....
....

Limitation 3: *Chlorine particles are not round.*

The student has omitted to describe how particles are represented in the particle theory. Sodium ions and chloride ions have not been included in the answer.

....
....

Quantitative chemistry

Find the answer

1 Use the mark scheme to find the answer that would be awarded 1 mark. Choose **A, B, C** or **D**. Explain your choice.

---

06 Calcium carbonate reacts with hydrochloric acid. The equation is:

$$CaCO_3(s) + 2HCl(aq) \rightarrow CaCl_2(aq) + H_2O(l) + CO_2(g)$$

25 g calcium carbonate is added to 36.5 g hydrochloric acid in a conical flask.

06.1 Which reactant is the limiting reactant? [1 mark]

Question	Answer	Mark
06.1	calcium carbonate	1

A — There is not enough calcium carbonate, so hydrochloric acid is the limiting reactant.

B — 25 g calcium carbonate reacts with 36.5 g hydrochloric acid, so there is not enough calcium carbonate to react with all the acid and calcium carbonate is the limiting reactant.

C — Only 27.75 g calcium chloride can be made.

D — There is too much acid and some will be left over.

> You only need to name the reactant to answer this question; you do not need to explain why, but if you do you will not lose any marks. You just waste a bit of time.

Answer .... would be awarded 1 mark because ....

....

....

---

2 Use the mark scheme to find the answer that would **not** be awarded 1 mark. Choose **A, B, C** or **D**. Explain your choice.

06.2 Students recorded the mass of the conical flask and contents during the reaction. The mass of the flask and contents decreased.

Explain why. [1 mark]

Question	Answer	Extra information	Mark
06.2	a gaseous product is formed	accept named product	1

A — Carbon dioxide is lost from the flask.

B — One of the products is a gas.

C — The flask did not have a stopper in it.

D — Carbon dioxide is a gas which escapes.

Answer .... would not be awarded 1 mark because ....

....

....

Quantitative chemistry

Complete the answer

1 Use the hint below to complete the student's answer so that it would be awarded 2 marks.

01 Some students prepared a series of sodium hydroxide (NaOH) solutions.

They dissolved 0.40 g sodium hydroxide in different volumes of water to make the solutions.

They then calculated the concentration of their solutions and recorded the results in **Table 5**.

01.1 Complete **Table 5**. The first concentration has been done for you. [2 marks]

Nearly there

Table 5

Volume of solution made in cm³	Concentration of solution in g per dm³
100	4.0
200	2.0
300	1.3
400	
500	

Hint
- Remember to use the same number of significant figures in your answers as used in the question.

2 Use the hints below to complete the student's answer so that it would be awarded 3 marks.

01.2 Plot the results in **Table 5** on the grid in **Figure 6**.

Draw a line of best fit. [3 marks]

Had a go

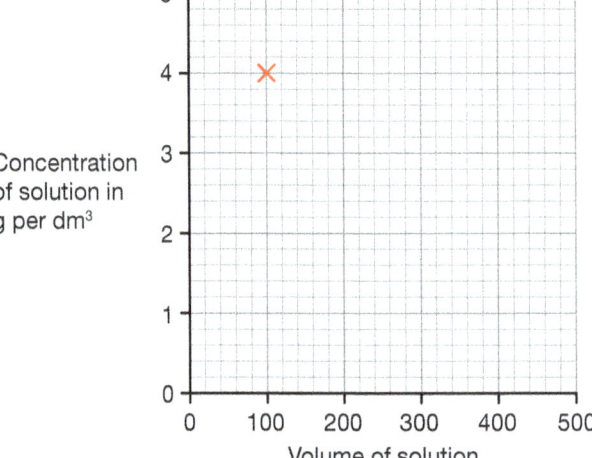

Figure 6

Hints
- Plot the data accurately.
- Do you expect any anomalous points?
- A line of best fit can be a straight line or a curve.

Chemical changes

Complete the question

1 Complete the question by adding **three** half equations in the boxes. Make sure two are correct.

02.1 Magnesium reacts with chlorine in a redox reaction.

The equation is: $Mg(s) + Cl_2(g) \rightarrow MgCl_2(s)$

Draw **two** lines to link the oxidation and reduction reactions to the correct half equations. **[2 marks]**

$Mg + 2e^- \rightarrow Mg^{2+}$

$Cl_2 \rightarrow 2Cl + 2e^-$

Oxidation reaction

Reduction reaction

Hints
- Work out what is oxidised and what is reduced first.
- Write the correct half equations before you write the incorrect options.
- Make your subscripts and superscripts clear.

Chemical changes

Improve the answer

1 Use the hint below to write an improved answer that would be awarded 2 marks.

05 Hydrochloric acid is a strong acid. **Table 6** shows how the hydrogen ion concentration of different strengths of hydrochloric acid is related to its pH.

Table 6

pH	Concentration of hydrogen ions in mol per dm³
1	0.1
2	0.01
3	0.001
4	0.0001
5	0.00001

Hint
- 0.1 is 1×10^{-1} in standard form, 0.01 is 1×10^{-2} and so on.

05.1 What is the relationship between the pH of hydrochloric acid and the hydrogen ion concentration? **[2 marks]**

Had a go

The pH increases by 1 each time the hydrogen ions go up by 0.1 and the number on the indices is the same as the pH.

....

....

Identify the trends in pH and hydrogen ion concentration first.

2 Use the hints below to write an improved answer that would be awarded 2 marks.

05.2 Ethanoic acid is a weak acid.

Explain why 0.1 mol per dm³ hydrochloric acid has a pH of 1, but 0.1 mol per dm³ ethanoic acid has a pH of 3.

[2 marks]

Had a go

The hydrogen ion concentration of pH 3 is 0.001. When the acid is weak, it is more diluted and there are fewer hydrogen ions in it.

Hints
- Do not confuse the terms strong and weak acids with concentrated and dilute acids.
- You may need to refer back to the information given at the beginning of the question. This is still part of question 5.

....

....

....

....

Re-order the answer

Chemical changes

1 Rearrange the sentences into the most logical order by numbering each part of the answer.

10 Students used the apparatus shown in **Figure 7** to pass electricity through sodium chloride solution.

A few drops of universal indicator were added to the sodium chloride solution.

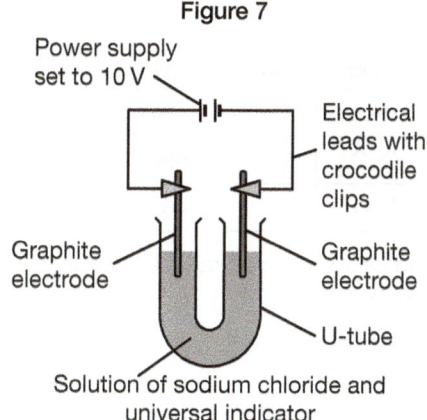

Figure 7

These were their observations after a few minutes:
- the indicator was bleached to colourless at the anode (positive electrode)
- the indicator turned purple at the cathode (negative electrode)
- the indicator stayed green at the bottom of the U-tube.

10.1 Explain the students' observations. **[5 marks]**

> **Hint**
> - The electrolysis of aqueous solutions such as sodium chloride solution is Required practical 9. You have probably carried out a similar experiment in your science lessons. You may have used different apparatus.

☐	The chlorine gas formed bleached the indicator to colourless.
☐	These formed an alkaline solution and the indicator turned purple.
☐	At the cathode, the reaction was $2H^+ + 2e^- \rightarrow H_2$.
☐	Hydrogen was given off and sodium ions and hydroxide ions remained in the solution.
☐	The reaction at the anode was $2Cl^- \rightarrow Cl_2 + 2e^-$.
☐	The indicator stayed green at the bottom of the tube because the ions did not have time to diffuse.

I would explain this to myself first, then match it to the statements.

Energy changes

Mark the answer

1 Draw lines to connect each of the marker's comments to the relevant part of the answer.

---

12 Hydrogen can be used as a fuel. The equation shows the bonds involved when hydrogen burns in oxygen.

$$2H\text{–}H + O=O \rightarrow 2H\text{–}O\text{–}H$$

Table 7 gives the bond energies for each of the bonds.

Table 7

Bond	Bond energy in kJ/mol
H–H	436
O=O	496
O–H	463

12.1 Use the equation and bond energies to calculate the overall energy change when 2 mol hydrogen burns in oxygen. Write your answers in the table below.

[5 marks]

Hint
- The question is asking for energy changes when 2 mol hydrogen reacts. Check how many moles of hydrogen react in the equation.

Bonds broken and energy absorbed in kJ/mol	
2 × H–H	2 × 436
O=O	496
Total	1368
Bonds made and energy released in kJ/mol	
2 × O–H	2 × 463
Total	926

Marker's comments:
- The energy absorbed when bonds are broken is correctly calculated.
- Bonds broken are correctly identified.
- This is correct for two O–H bonds, but not for four. Error is carried forward.
- The number of O–H bonds broken is incorrect here. Four O–H bonds are broken.

Overall energy change: when 2 mol hydrogen burns = 926 − 1368 = **−442** kJ/mol

---

2 Now use the mark scheme below to decide how many marks you would award the answer. Give reasons for your mark.

Question	Answer	Extra information	Mark
12.1	bonds broken = 2 × H–H; 1 × O = O	allow ecf	1
	bonds made = 4 × O–H		1
	energy absorbed when bonds broken = (2 × 436) + 496 = 1368		1
	energy released when bonds are made = 4 × 463 = 1852		1
	overall energy change = 1852 − 1368 = 484		1

Hint
- 'ecf' means 'error carried forward'. If you make a mistake early in the calculation and get an incorrect answer, but your method is correct, you only lose the mark once.

I would award the answer .... out of 5 marks because ....

....

....

Find the answer

1 Use the mark scheme to find the answer that would **not** be awarded 2 marks.
Choose **A**, **B** or **C**. Explain your choice.

07 In **Figure 8**, Reaction profile A shows an exothermic reaction; Reaction profile B shows an endothermic reaction.

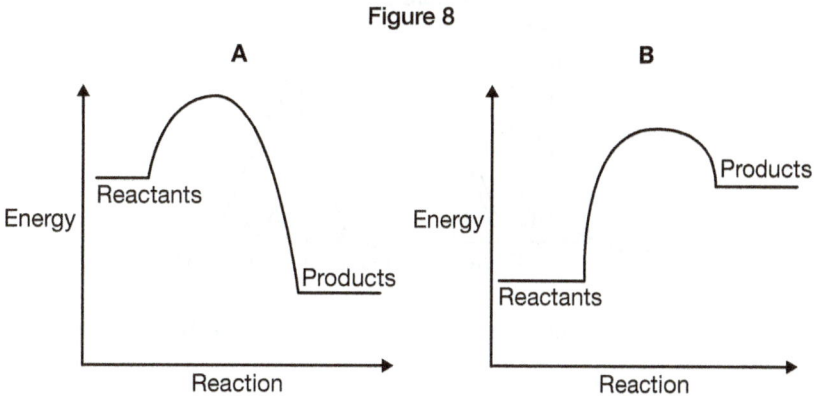

Figure 8

07.1 Describe the difference between the energy released in forming new bonds and the energy needed to break existing bonds for the two reaction profiles. [2 marks]

Question	Answer	Extra information	Mark
07.1	in A, the energy released when new bonds are formed is greater than the energy needed to break existing bonds	allow converse answers	1
	in B, the energy released when new bonds are formed is less than the energy needed to break existing bonds		1

Hint
- Here, 'converse' means the other way round. So, 'In A, the energy needed to break existing bonds is less than the energy given out when new bonds form' means the same as in the mark scheme and is a correct answer.

A More energy is given out when new bonds are made in exothermic reactions than is absorbed when old bonds are broken. In endothermic reactions, less energy is given out when new bonds form than is needed to break the old ones.

B More energy is given out when bonds form than when they break. For the other one, less energy is given out when bonds form than is needed to break them.

C In B, the energy needed to break old bonds is more than the energy given out when new bonds form. In A, the energy needed to break old bonds is less than the energy given out when new bonds are made.

Answer .... would not be awarded 2 marks because
....
....

The rate and extent of chemical change

Complete the question

1 Complete the question by adding **two** multiple-choice options. Make sure one is correct.

09 A student has used the apparatus in **Figure 9** to investigate the rate of the reaction between magnesium ribbon and dilute hydrochloric acid.

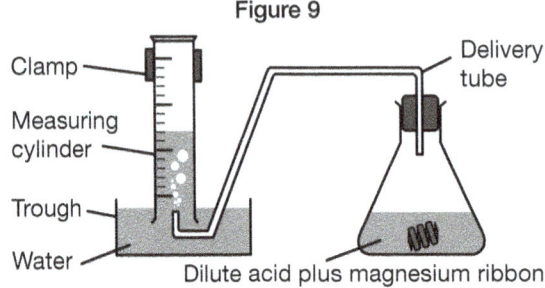

Figure 9

They have recorded the volume of hydrogen given off at 10 s intervals. **Figure 10** shows their results plotted on a graph. The student has drawn a tangent at 40 s.

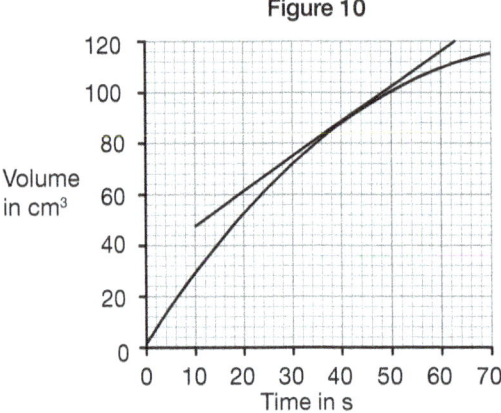

Figure 10

Hint
- Don't forget to include the units.

09.1 What is the rate of reaction at 40 s, to two significant figures?

Tick **one** box. [1 mark]

0.71 cm³/s ☐

1.35 cm³/s ☐

.... ☐

.... ✓

Work out the correct answer first, then decide where mistakes could be made to think of an incorrect answer.

The rate and extent of chemical change

Improve the answer

1 Use the marker's comments below to write an improved answer that would be awarded 2 marks.

06 Hydrogen and nitrogen react together to produce ammonia. The equation is:

$$3H_2(g) + N_2(g) \rightleftharpoons 2NH_3(g)$$

The reaction is reversible. The reaction to produce ammonia is exothermic.

06.1 Describe the effect of increasing the pressure on the position of the equilibrium and the amount of ammonia formed. [2 marks]

Had a go

Increasing the pressure pushes all the molecules closer together and there are more collisions, so more NH_3 is formed.

- This is collision theory and not directly relevant to the question.
- This part is correct, but no correct explanation is given.

It is sometimes fine to use formulae in an answer, as long as the formulae are correct. You will lose marks if you get them wrong. It is safer to use chemical names in explanations.

2 Use the marker's comments below to write an improved answer that would be awarded 2 marks.

06.2 What effect does increasing the temperature have on the position of equilibrium and the amount of ammonia formed? [2 marks]

Had a go

The reaction is exothermic, so heat energy is given out. When the temperature is increased, it moves to absorb the extra heat and less NH_2 is made.

- The student has not been clear what 'it' refers to.
- The formula for ammonia is incorrect; no marks here.
- Scientific language is generally lacking.

Remember to refer to the equation at the beginning of the question if you need to.

Organic chemistry

Complete the answer

1 Use the hints below to complete the student's answer so that it would be awarded 2 marks.

04 **Figure 11** shows the displayed formula of methane.

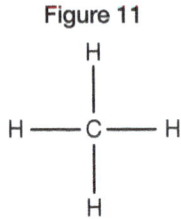

Figure 11

04.1 Draw a similar diagram for propane, C_3H_8. [2 marks]

Had a go

C—C—C

Hints
- Displayed formulae show all the bonds and symbols for all the atoms.
- Make sure your bond lines are accurately placed.

2 Use the hints below to complete the student's answer so that it would be awarded 2 marks.

04.2 Propane is used as a fuel. Balance the equation to show propane reacting with oxygen. [2 marks]

Had a go

$C_3H_8(g) + \ldots O_2(g) \rightarrow \ldots H_2O(g) + \underline{3} CO_2(g)$

Hints
- You can only change the prefix numbers when balancing equations; you must not change the subscripts.
- Count all the elements on both sides of the equation first, then balance the element with the greatest number of atoms, and adjust from there.

3 Complete the student's answer so that it would be awarded 4 marks.

04.3 Describe **two** chemical tests and their results to identify the products from the combustion of propane. [4 marks]

Had a go

Test 1: The products can be bubbled through limewater. ....

....

Test 2: ....

....

Mark the answer

1 Use the mark scheme below to decide how many marks you would award the answer. Give reasons for your mark.

12 **Figure 12** shows a fractional distillation column. It is used to separate the hydrocarbons in crude oil into fractions. Most of the hydrocarbons in crude oil are alkanes.

Figure 12

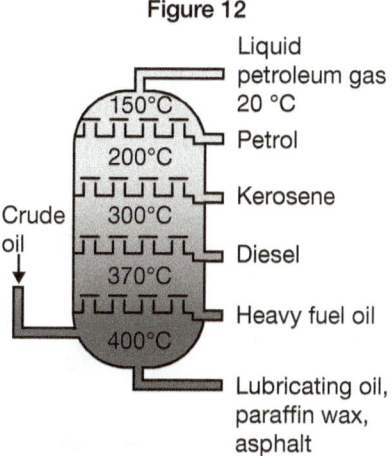

12.1 Explain why the alkanes in liquid petroleum gas rise further up the fractionating column than the alkanes in petrol. Your answer should include ideas about intermolecular forces.

[6 marks]

Crude oil is a mixture of different-sized alkanes. The alkanes in liquid petroleum gas are smaller than those in petrol. Smaller alkanes have lower boiling points because they have fewer intermolecular forces to break to boil. Gaseous hydrocarbons enter the bottom of the fractionating column and rise up it. The temperature decreases the further up the fractionating column you go until you get to the boiling point and the fractions are collected.

Level	Answer	Mark
3	A logical answer including the nature of the alkanes, their difference in boiling points explained and separation in the fractionating column. Comparisons made between the hydrocarbons in liquid petroleum gas and petrol.	5–6
2	Most relevant points are included, but detail may be lacking. The explanation may not be logical. Some comparisons are made.	3–4
1	Simple statements are made with no comparisons. There are some relevant points, but the answer would not lead to understanding.	1–2
	No relevant content.	0

Indicative content
- alkanes in LPG are smaller than the alkanes in petrol
- smaller alkanes have lower boiling points
- smaller alkanes have fewer intermolecular forces between molecules; less energy is needed to break them and boiling point is lower
- there is a temperature gradient in the fractionating column
- gaseous alkanes rise up the fractionating column and condense when they reach their boiling point

I would award the answer   out of 6 marks because

Chemical analysis

Re-order the answer

1 Rearrange the working out into the most logical order by numbering each part of the answer.

06 Some students have prepared the chromatogram shown in **Figure 13**.

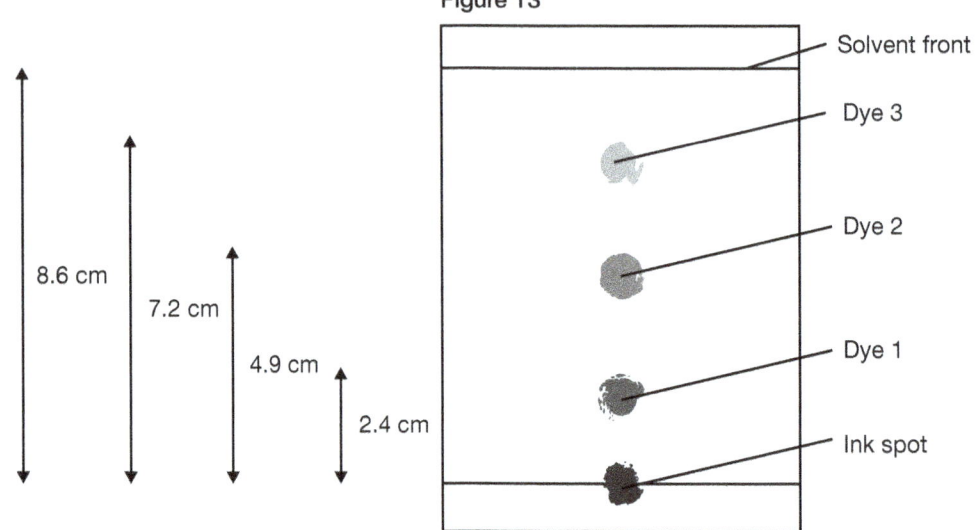

06.3 Calculate the R_f value of dye 1, dye 2 and dye 3.

Give your answers to two significant figures. [4 marks]

Hints

If you have to calculate R_f values, remember:
- you cannot have an answer greater than 1
- measure the distances from the **centre** of each spot to the base line.

☐ = 0.28

☐ R_f dye 3 = $\frac{7.2}{8.6}$

☐ R_f dye 2 = $\frac{4.9}{8.6}$

☐ = 0.57

☐ R_f dye 1 = $\frac{2.4}{8.6}$

☐ R_f = $\frac{\text{distance moved by spot}}{\text{distance moved by solvent}}$

☐ = 0.84

> Paper chromatography is Required practical 12. You have probably carried out this experiment in class. Try to think back to what you did.

Chemical analysis

Find the answer

1 Use the mark scheme to find the answer that would **not** be awarded 2 marks. Explain your choice.

01.2 A student investigated changes in boiling point when sodium chloride was dissolved in water. This was their method:
- Measure 100 cm^3 distilled water (pure water).
- Heat the water until it boils and measure the boiling point.
- Remove the water from the heat source; add 1 g of sodium chloride and stir to dissolve.
- Heat the salt solution and measure its boiling point.
- Continue adding 1 g lots of sodium chloride and measuring the boiling point.

The student's results are given in **Table 8**.

Table 8

Mass of salt added in g	0	1.0	2.0	3.0	4.0	5.0	6.0
Boiling point in °C	100.0	100.2	100.4	100.6	100.8	101.0	101.2

Identify **two** conclusions the student could make. [2 marks]

Question	Answer	Extra information	Mark
01.2	any **two** from: • adding sodium chloride to pure water increases the boiling point • the boiling point of sodium chloride solution increases by 0.2 °C for every gram of sodium chloride added (for this range) • the boiling point of sodium chloride solution depends on the mass of sodium chloride dissolved • the boiling point of sodium chloride solution is directly proportional to the mass of sodium chloride dissolved (for this range)	allow other correct answers	2

A The boiling point rises by 0.2 °C for every 1 g sodium chloride dissolved. 6 g sodium chloride is the maximum that can dissolve in 100 cm^3 water.

B Sodium chloride solution has a higher boiling point than pure water. The boiling point of sodium chloride solution rises as the concentration increases.

C The boiling point increases when sodium chloride is added to water. Every time 1 g sodium chloride is added, the boiling point goes up 0.2 °C.

Answer .... would not be awarded 2 marks because
....
....
....

> Conclusions must be based on the evidence given in the question, not on anything else you might know.

Chemical analysis

Complete the answer

1 Complete the student's answer so that it would be awarded 3 marks.

---

08 Pure gold is too soft for making everyday jewellery. Most 'gold' jewellery is made from gold alloys.

Jewellers use two methods to measure the purity of gold:
- carats: 24 carat gold is pure gold
- fineness: parts per thousand of gold.

08.1 Complete **Table 9**. One line has been done for you. **[3 marks]**

Had a go

Table 9

Percentage of gold in %	Carat	Fineness
100	24	1000
75		
50	12	500
37.5		

---

2 Use the hints below to complete the student's answer so that it would be awarded 2 marks.

08.2 Explain why 24 carat gold is a pure substance, but 9 carat gold is a formulated product. **[2 marks]**

Had a go

24 carat gold only contains gold atoms ....

....

....

Hints
- You probably have not learned about gold in your science lessons, but you have learned about the scientific ideas you need to answer this question.
- Here, the examiner is testing whether you can apply your scientific ideas to a different context (gold).

Remember that 'Explain' is a command word. You need to make something clear or give reasons for something happening.

---

3 Complete the student's answer so that it would be awarded 2 marks.

08.3 Explain why 9 carat gold is harder than pure gold. **[2 marks]**

Had a go

The atoms in pure gold are all the same size ....

....

....

Make sure your answer is a comparison and mentions both types of gold.

46

Chemistry of the atmosphere

Complete the question

1 Complete the question by adding **two** multiple-choice options. Make sure one is correct.

04.1 A sample of coal contains these elements:

| carbon | oxygen | hydrogen | nitrogen | sulfur |

The coal burns in a **limited** air supply. Predict **two** atmospheric pollutants that could be produced.

Tick **one** box. [1 mark]

.... ✓

.... ☐

Water and carbon monoxide ☐

Sulfur dioxide and water ☐

I would choose non-polluting atmospheric gases for the incorrect options. This will really test whether the student has understood the question properly.

2 Use the hints and answer below to complete the question.

05 Methane is a greenhouse gas. **Figure 14** shows changes in the amount of atmospheric methane.

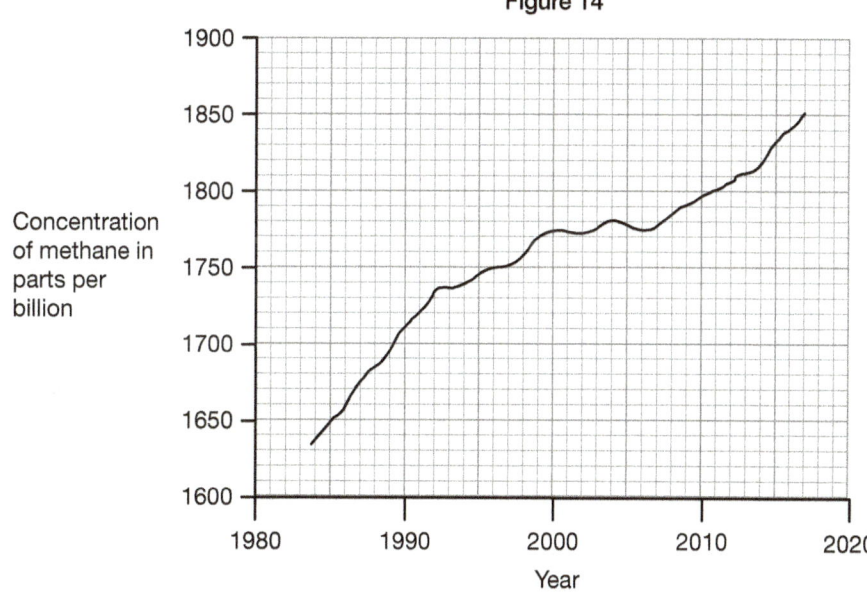

Figure 14

05.1 Calculate ....

.... [2 marks]

Nailed it!

2016 − 1984 = 32

1840 − 1640 = 200

$\dfrac{200}{32} = 6.25$

.... 6.25 .... parts per billion

Hints
- First, find the numbers that appear in the calculation on the graph.
- When you've written the question, answer it yourself to check it's correct.

Chemistry of the atmosphere

Find the answer

1 Use the mark scheme to find the answer that would **not** be awarded 2 marks. Choose **A, B, C** or **D**. Explain your choice.

---

07 The carbon footprint of one pair of jeans is calculated to be 33.44 kg carbon dioxide and other greenhouse gases.

This includes the following contributors:
- growing and harvesting the cotton
- producing the denim fabric
- manufacturing the jeans
- all transport and energy
- use of the jeans (washing etc.)
- disposal of the jeans

07.1 Identify **two** ways in which the carbon footprint can be reduced. [2 marks]

Question	Answer	Extra information	Mark
07.1	any **two** from: • strategies to use alternative energy sources • energy saving strategies • strategies to reduce transport • washing less frequently • recycling	allow specific answers allow other correct answers	2

A — Use solar power to provide the electricity and wear the jeans for longer before washing them.

B — Use natural gas instead of coal or oil to provide the energy. Natural gas does not produce carbon dioxide when burned.

C — Manufacture the jeans where the cotton is grown and use hydroelectric power to provide the energy.

D — Wash the jeans at a lower temperature and send them to a charity shop when you have finished with them.

> Read all the answers before deciding which one would **not** get 2 marks.

Answer .... would not be awarded 2 marks because ....

....

....

....

Hints
- Remember that the carbon footprint involves the full life cycle of a product.
- There are many correct answers to this question. The mark scheme only gives a few.

Chemistry of the atmosphere

Re-order the answer

1 Rearrange the sentences below into the most logical order by numbering each part of the answer.

01 Evidence shows that the Earth is 4.6 billion years old.

There are several theories about how the Earth's atmosphere formed and has changed over time.

01.1 Describe **one** theory about how the Earth's atmosphere has changed over 4.6 billion years. [5 marks]

- [ ] The water vapour condensed to form the oceans.
- [ ] Plants evolved and used carbon dioxide in photosynthesis, releasing oxygen.
- [ ] There was intense volcanic activity during the first one billion years.
- [ ] Some carbon dioxide dissolved in the oceans, reducing the amount in the atmosphere.
- [ ] This produced an early atmosphere of mainly carbon dioxide and water vapour, with some nitrogen.
- [ ] The percentage of oxygen in the atmosphere allowed animals to evolve.

Think of the events as a timeline. Make the sentences tell a story.

2 Rearrange the sentences below into the most logical order by numbering each part of the answer.

01.2 Some scientists think that the evidence for the Earth's early atmosphere containing mostly carbon dioxide and water vapour is weak.

Explain why scientists might think this. [3 marks]

- [ ] Therefore ideas are often modelled on similar events that happen today.
- [ ] However, conditions were very different billions of years ago and this might not be true.
- [ ] Collecting evidence for events that happened billions of years ago is difficult.
- [ ] We assume the composition of volcanic gases was the same billions of years ago as it is today.

Using resources

Mark the answer

1 Draw lines to connect each of the marker's comments to the relevant part of the answer.

---

11 We are running out of high-grade copper ores. Areas where copper ores were once quarried still contain low-grade copper ores.

Table 10 gives some information about two methods that can be used to extract copper from low-grade ores.

Table 10

	Phytomining	Bioleaching
Method	Plants are grown in soil containing low-grade copper ore. The plants are harvested and burned. The ash contains copper compounds.	Bacteria are used to absorb copper compounds in low-grade ores. A leach solution is produced containing copper compounds.
Extracting the copper	Displacement with scrap iron or electrolysis	Displacement with scrap iron or electrolysis
Time span	A growing season	2 years

11.1 Evaluate the environmental impact of using phytomining and bioleaching to extract copper from low-grade ores. **[6 marks]**

Both methods extract the copper using scrap iron or by electrolysis, so they both need energy to do that. That usually means using fossil fuels which might run out. Growing plants on copper soils is like ordinary farming and is better to look at than mines. But the plants have to be burnt which uses electricity. Bioleaching does not need burning, but it takes a long time. The burning might give off polluting gases.

Marker's comments:
- Question does not ask for comparisons with traditional mining.
- Similar environmental impacts of both methods are identified.
- Carbon dioxide and water given off; carbon dioxide is a greenhouse gas, but is not polluting.
- A valid comparison is made.
- No comparison is made.

This question continues on page 51.

> 'Evaluate' is a command word. You should use the information given in the question, as well as your own knowledge to consider evidence for and against.

Using resources

Improve the answer

1 On page 50, there is a question comparing phytomining and bioleaching. You have looked at one student's answer to this question. Write an improved answer that would be awarded 6 marks.

....
....
....
....
....
....
....
....
....
....

2 Write an improved answer that would be awarded 4 marks.

11.2 In Europe, 40% of the copper used is now produced from recycled copper.

Table 11 gives the energy requirements of each process.

Table 11

Source of copper	Energy needed to produce 1 tonne in GJ/tonne
Traditional mining	100
Recycled copper	10

Identify **two** advantages to the environment in using recycled copper rather than new copper produced by traditional mining. Explain your answer.

[4 marks]

Had a go

Advantage 1: Recycled copper is cheaper than new copper because it doesn't use so much energy.

Explanation: Energy is expensive.

Advantage 2: Recycled copper will not end up in landfill, but new copper might.

Explanation: We would need fewer landfill sites.

Advantage 1: ....

Explanation: ....
....
....

Advantage 2: ....

Explanation: ....
....

Energy

Complete the answer

1 Complete the student's answer so that it would be awarded 2 marks.

06 **Figure 15** shows an electric kettle.

Figure 15

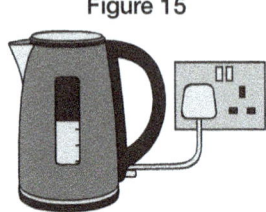

06.1 Complete the sentences. Use words from the box. [2 marks]

| energy | minute | heat | ~~second~~ | time |

Nearly there

The power of the kettle is the rate at which it transfers …………………………. It is measured in watts.

An energy transfer of one joule per …*second*……. is equal to a power of 1 watt.

> You must make sure you learn the units that quantities are measured in, such as energy being measured in joules.

2 Use the hint below to complete the student's answer so that it would be awarded 4 marks.

09.2 Water has a specific heat capacity of 4 200 J/kg °C.

Calculate the change in thermal energy when 0.1 kg of water is heated from 20 °C to 40 °C. [4 marks]

Had a go

$\Delta E = m\, c\, \Delta\theta$ ……………………………………………………………………………………

………

………

………

Change in thermal energy = …………………… J

> **Hint**
> - The equation you will need is:
>   change in thermal energy = mass × specific heat capacity × temperature change.
>   In the exam, you will have to choose the correct equation from the Physics Equation Sheet.

Mark the answer

1 Draw lines to connect each of the marker's comments to the relevant part of the answer.

> 04   Figure 16 shows a person holding a stone.
>
> Figure 16
>
>
>
> **04.1** Describe the changes to energy stores when the stone is dropped and allowed to fall. **[3 marks]**
>
> Before the stone is dropped, all the energy is in the gravitational potential store. It then falls and loses this energy.
>
> — The correct energy store has been identified.
> — The changes to named stores are not described.

2 Now use the mark scheme below to decide how many marks you would award the answer. Give reasons for your mark.

Question	Answer	Mark
04.1	before the stone is released, it has a store of gravitational potential energy	1
	when it is falling, the stone's store of kinetic energy increases	1
	and the stone's store of gravitational potential energy decreases	1

I would award the answer .... out of 3 marks because ....

....

....

Energy

Complete the question

1 Use the student's answer below to complete the question.

06 **Figure 17** shows condensation on a shower screen.

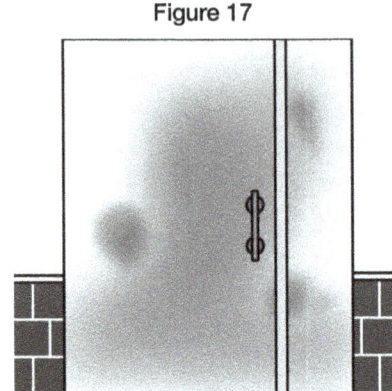

Figure 17

The density of water = ... kg/m³

A volume of .... of condensation forms on the screen.

The specific latent heat of vaporisation of water = 2.26×10^6 J/kg.

06.1 Use this information to calculate the energy released when the condensation forms. **[5 marks]**

> Work out the mass of condensation before calculating the energy released.

Nailed it!

Density = mass ÷ volume, so mass = density × volume

mass = $1000 \times 3.0 \times 10^{-5}$ = 0.03 kg

Energy = mass × specific latent heat of vaporisation

Energy = $0.03 \times 2.26 \times 10^6$ = 67 800

Energy released = ...67 800............ J

> Here, the first marking point is for rearranging density = mass ÷ volume; the second is for correct substitution; the third is for correctly calculating the mass; the fourth is for correct substitution into $E = m\,l$; the fifth is for the correct final answer.

2 Complete the question by adding **two** multiple-choice options. Make sure one is correct.

07.4 Which of the following is a correct rearrangement of the equation used to calculate the amount of kinetic energy an object has?

Tick **one** box. **[1 mark]**

.... ☐

.... ✓

$E_k \times v^2 = \dfrac{1}{2} \times m$ ☐

$v = \dfrac{(2E_k)}{m^2}$ ☐

54

Energy

Find the answer

1 Use the mark scheme to find the answer that would **not** be awarded 3 marks. Choose **A, B or C**.

02.3 The specific heat capacity of water is 4200 J/kg °C.

Calculate the change in thermal energy when 4 kg of water is heated from 60 °C to 85 °C. **[3 marks]**

Question	Answer	Mark
02.3	$\Delta\theta$ = 25 °C	1
	ΔE = 4 × 4200 × 25	1
	= 420 000 J	1

A $E = 4200 \times 4 \times 25 = 420000\,J$

B The change in thermal energy = mass × temperature = 4 × 85 = 340 J

C Energy change = mass × specific heat capacity × change in temperature
Mass = 4 kg; SHC = 4200 J/kg °C;
temperature change = 85 − 60 = 25 °C
Energy change = 4 × 4200 × 25 = 420000 J

Hint
- You need to use the change in temperature to calculate the change in thermal energy. The equation you will need is: **change in thermal energy = mass × specific heat capacity × temperature change.** In the exam, you will have to choose the correct equation from the Physics Equation Sheet.

Answer .... would not be awarded 3 marks because ....

....

2 Use the mark scheme to find the answer that would **not** be awarded any marks. Choose **A, B or C**.

03.4 A car of mass 1500 kg is travelling at a speed of 12 m/s.

Calculate the kinetic energy of the car. **[3 marks]**

Question	Answer	Mark
03.4	$E_k = \frac{1}{2}mv^2$	1
	$E_k = \frac{1}{2} \times 1500 \times 12^2$	1
	= 108 000 J	1

A Kinetic energy = 108 J

B Kinetic energy = $\frac{1}{2}mv^2 = \frac{1}{2} \times 12^2 \times 1500 = 108\,000$ joules = 108 kJ

C $E_k = 0.5 \times 1500 \times (12)^2 = 108\,000\,J$

Answer .... would not be awarded any marks because ....

....

....

Electricity

Re-order the answer

1 Rearrange the sentences into the most logical order by numbering each part of the answer.

07.1 A student sets up a circuit containing a power supply, ammeter, voltmeter and a length of wire. He uses it to investigate how the length of the wire affects its resistance.

Describe a method he could follow in order to do this. **[4 marks]**

- [ ] Repeat for 5 different lengths of wire.
- [ ] Record the readings on the ammeter and voltmeter.
- [ ] Measure the length of wire and record it.
- [ ] Calculate the resistance using $R = V \div I$ and plot a graph of resistance against length.

> **When you are asked a question about a required practical, think back to what you did when you carried out the experiment.**

Hint
- Make sure the order of your method makes sense when you read it back.

2 Rearrange the working into the most logical order by numbering each part of the answer.

09.1 A kettle has a power rating of 2.5 kW. The mains supply is 230 V. The current is 10.9 A.

Calculate the resistance of the element in the kettle. **[4 marks]**

- [ ] $R = 21.0\,\Omega$
- [ ] so $R = P \div I^2$
- [ ] $R = 2500 \div 10.9^2$
- [ ] $P = I^2 R$

Mark the answer

1 Use the mark scheme below to decide how many marks you would award the answer.
Give reasons for your mark.

---

03 A student sets up the circuit shown in **Figure 18**.

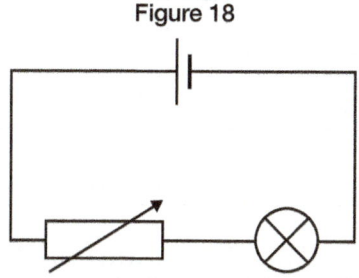

Figure 18

When the potential difference across the lamp is 3.0 V, the current is 0.10 A.

03.1 Write down the equation that links current, potential difference and resistance. [1 mark]

P.d = resistance × current

Question	Answer	Mark
03.1	potential difference = current × resistance	1

I would award the answer .... out of 1 mark because

....

---

2 Use the mark scheme below to decide how many marks you would award the answer.
Give reasons for your mark.

03.2 Calculate the resistance of the lamp. [3 marks]

Resistance = potential difference ÷ current

R = 3.0 ÷ 0.10

Resistance = ...*3*........ Ω

Question	Answer	Mark
03.2	resistance = potential difference ÷ current	1
	R = 3.0 ÷ 0.10 (Ω)	1
	R = 30 (Ω)	1

I would award the answer .... out of 3 marks because

....

....

Electricity

Improve the answer

1 Use the hint below to write an improved answer that would be awarded 3 marks.

04.5 Complete **Table 12** by writing down the function of the live wire, earth wire and neutral wire in a 3-core cable. **[3 marks]**

Nearly there

Table 12

Wire	Function
Live	This wire carries a high voltage in and around the home
Earth	This wire keeps us safe
Neutral	This wire provides a return path to the substation

Hint
- When you are asked for the function of a component, be sure to state the function itself, and not the effect of the function.

Wire	Function

---

2 Write an improved answer that would be awarded 3 marks.

05.1 Calculate the energy transferred by a 40 W light bulb in 3 minutes. **[3 marks]**

....

Energy transferred = ...**7200**........ J

> This student has correctly answered the question, but hasn't shown her working out.

....

....

Energy transferred = ... J

58

Complete the question

1 Complete the question by adding **three** multiple-choice options. Make sure two are correct.

06.3 Which two features of a graph, when combined, show that the quantities plotted are directly proportional?

Tick **two** boxes. [2 marks]

> **Hint**
> - The options given below show two incorrect features. Use them to help you work out the correct answers.

.... ✓

Line does not pass through the origin ☐

.... ✓

.... ☐

A curved line ☐

---

2 Use the hint and the student's answer below to complete the question.

05.6 A 3 Ω and a .... Ω resistor are connected in series with a 1.5 V battery.

Calculate the .... in the circuit. [3 marks]

> **Hint**
> - You need to use an equation that links current, potential difference and resistance.

Nailed it!

For resistors in series, the total resistance is the sum of the individual resistances of the resistors, so R_{total} = 3 + 7 = 10 Ω

$V = I \times R$, so $I = V \div R$

$I = 1.5 \div 10 = 0.15$ A

........0.15........ A

> You may be awarded marks for your working out, even if your answer is incorrect.

Particle model of matter

Complete the answer

1 Use the student's plan to write an answer that would be awarded 6 marks.

09 **Figure 19** shows a helium-filled balloon and a wooden block.

Figure 19

Balloon filled with helium   Wooden block

Solids are difficult to compress and have a fixed shape but gases can be easily compressed and take the shape of their container.

09.1 Use your knowledge of kinetic theory to explain these properties of solids and gases. **[6 marks]**

Had a go

Plan: consider – movement of particles in solids and gases; spacing between the particles in solids and gases; forces between particles in solids and gases

2 Complete the student's answer so that it would be awarded 3 marks.

06.5 Calculate the mass of air in a room which measures 6 m by 5 m by 4 m.
The density of air is 1.3 kg/m³. **[3 marks]**

Had a go

$\rho = m \div V$; $V = 6 \times 5 \times 4 = 120 \, m^3$

Mass of air = ... kg

Particle model of matter

Find the answer

1 Use the mark scheme to find the answer that would **not** be awarded 1 mark. Choose **A, B or C**. Explain your choice.

04.1 The particle model can be used to explain the properties of solids.

Describe the motion of the particles in a solid. **[1 mark]**

Question	Answer	Mark
04.1	the particles vibrate **but** do not change their positions	1

A The particles don't swap places, but they do vibrate where they are.

B The particles vibrate to and fro.

C The particles all vibrate but they cannot change position.

You must be specific when answering questions like this.

Answer .... would not be awarded 1 mark because ....

....

---

2 Use the mark scheme to find the **two** answers that would **not** be awarded 2 marks. Choose two from **A, B, C or D**. Explain your choices.

06.4 Calculate the mass of an iron block with a volume of 3 m^3.

The density of iron is 8000 kg/m^3. **[2 marks]**

Question	Answer	Mark
06.4	mass = density × volume	1
	mass = 8000 (kg/m^3) × 3 (m^3) = 24 000 kg	1

A 24 000 g

B d = mass ÷ vol. So mass = 8000 ÷ 3 = 24 kg

C m = ρV; m = 8000 × 3 = 2.4 × 10^4 kg

D m = ρV; m = 8000 × 3 = 24 000 kg

Answers .... and .... would not be awarded 2 marks because ....

....

....

....

61

Particle model of matter

Improve the answer

1 Use the hint below to write an improved answer that would be awarded 3 marks.

> **09.1** Use the particle model to explain why a gas exerts a pressure on its container. **[3 marks]**
>
> **Had a go**
>
> There are particles in the gas and they bump into each other and hit the walls of the container.
>
> **Hint**
> - An explanation usually contains more than one statement linked together.
>
> ....
> ....
> ....
>
> *If the question is worth 3 marks, you will need to make three distinct points to be awarded full marks.*

2 Use the hint below to write an improved answer that would be awarded 4 marks.

> **14** The specific latent heat of fusion = 340 000 J/kg. The specific latent heat of vaporisation = 2 260 000 J/kg. The specific heat capacity of water is 4200 J/kg °C.
>
> Calculate the total energy transferred when 500 g of ice cubes at 0 °C are changed into steam at 100 °C. **[4 marks]**
>
> **Had a go**
>
> Total energy transferred = ...1 510 000..... J
>
> **Hint**
> - You should always show your working out. That way, you might still get a mark, even if your answer is wrong.
>
> ....
> ....
> ....
> ....
>
> Total energy transferred = ... J

Re-order the answer

1 Rearrange the sentences into the most logical order by numbering each part of the answer. One has been done for you.

06 A student wants to calculate the density of the two objects shown in **Figure 20**.

Figure 20

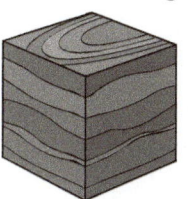 

When you are asked a question about a required practical, try to think back to what you did when you carried out the experiment.

06.1 Describe how she could do this. [4 marks]

- [ ] First, to calculate the volume of the block, measure the length of the sides of the cube with a ruler and calculate the volume using length × height × width.

- [1] Measure the mass of both objects using a balance.

- [ ] Calculate the density of both objects using density = mass ÷ volume.

- [ ] To determine the volume of the set of keys, immerse them in water and measure the volume of water displaced. This is equal to the volume of the set of keys.

2 Rearrange the sentences into the most logical order by numbering each part of the answer.

08.4 Describe the changes in temperature and state when a substance changes from a solid to a liquid and then to a gas. [3 marks]

- [ ] At its boiling point, the temperature of the substance stays the same until all of the substance has turned into a gas. The temperature then begins to rise again. The mass remains constant throughout.

- [ ] At its melting point, the temperature of the substance stays the same until it has all melted. The temperature of the liquid substance then rises again until it starts to change to a gas.

- [ ] When a solid is heated, its temperature rises until it begins to change to a liquid.

Once you have answered a question like this, read your answer back in the order you have suggested to make sure it makes sense.

Atomic structure

Improve the answer

1 Write an improved answer that would be awarded 2 marks.

02.2 Use **Figure 21** to determine the half-life of the radioisotope.

Show clearly on **Figure 21** how you worked it out. [2 marks]

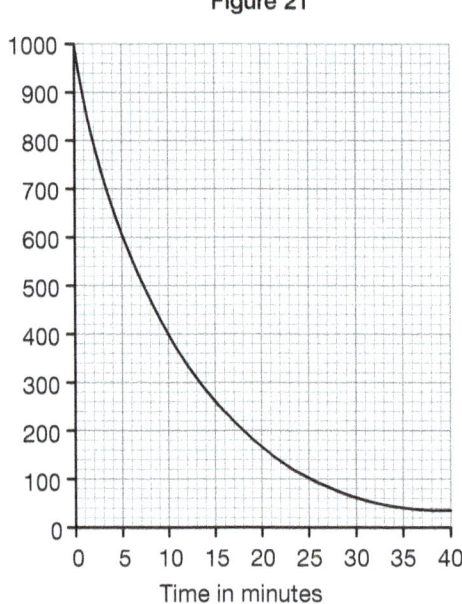

Figure 21

The student has correctly stated the half-life but has not shown on the graph how he determined the value.

Nearly there

Half-life = 7.5 minutes

....
....
....

2 Use the hint below to write an improved answer that would be awarded 4 marks.

08.5 Compare the ionising and penetrating power of the three types of nuclear radiation. [4 marks]

Had a go

Gamma is the most penetrating, then beta and alpha is the least penetrating.

> **Hint**
> - Extended answers should have a logical structure, and related points should be linked.

....
....
....
....
....
....

64

Atomic structure

Complete the answer

1 Complete the student's answer so that it would be awarded 2 marks.

> **04.6** Write a nuclear equation to show the radioactive decay of uranium-238, which emits an alpha particle. **[2 marks]**
>
> *Nearly there*
>
> An alpha particle is a helium nucleus, so has a mass number of 4 and an atomic number of 2.

Remember that the mass numbers must add up to the same number on both sides of the equation. The same is true for the atomic numbers.

2 Complete the student's answer so that it would be awarded 2 marks.

> **03.1** Write a nuclear equation to show the radioactive decay of carbon-15, which emits a beta particle. **[2 marks]**
>
> *Nearly there*
>
> A beta particle is a fast-moving electron, so has a mass number of 0 and an atomic number of −1.

3 Complete the student's answer so that it would be awarded 3 marks.

> **05.2** A radioisotope has a half-life of 15 days. A sample of this radioisotope has an activity of 640 Bq.
> Calculate the net decline after 60 days by completing **Table 13** below. **[3 marks]**
>
> *Nearly there*
>
> Table 13
>
> | Number of half-lives | Number of days | Total remaining | Fraction remaining |
> |---|---|---|---|
> | 0 | 0 | 640 | |
> | 1 | 15 | 320 | |
> | 2 | 30 | | |
> | 3 | 45 | | |
> | 4 | 60 | | |
>
> 60 days is equivalent to 4 half-lives.

65

Atomic structure

Complete the question

1 Complete the question by adding **three** multiple-choice options. Make sure two are correct.

05.4 Which **two** statements correctly describe the process of beta decay?

Tick **two** boxes. [2 marks]

> **Hints**
> - A beta particle is an electron.
> - Think about where this electron comes from.

In beta decay, a neutron is emitted from the nucleus. ☐

.... ✓

When a beta particle is emitted, the number of nucleons decreases by four. ☐

.... ✓

.... ☐

---

2 Complete the question by adding **three** multiple-choice options. Make sure two are correct.

06.2 Which **two** statements correctly describe gamma rays?

Tick **two** boxes. [2 marks]

.... ✓

Gamma rays have a relative mass of 1 but carry no charge. ☐

.... ✓

.... ☐

Gamma rays have no mass, but carry a negative charge. ☐

Re-order the answer

1 Rearrange the working out into the most logical order by numbering each part of the answer.

07.3 Calculate the momentum of a golf ball of mass 45 g travelling at 95 m/s. **[4 marks]**

> **Hint**
> - For calculation questions, always make sure that you begin by writing out the equation before substituting the numbers into the equation.

- ☐ Momentum = 0.045 × 95
- ☐ Mass = 45 ÷ 1000 = 0.045 kg
- ☐ Momentum = 4.275 kg m/s
- ☐ Momentum = mass × velocity

Always check the units for each quantity you are given in the question. Convert any that are not given in SI units before you use them.

2 Rearrange the sentences into the most logical order by numbering each part of the answer.

05.1 A student investigated the effect of force on the extension of a spring.
Describe a method they could follow in order to do this. **[4 marks]**

- ☐ Repeat by adding more masses, measuring the length and recording the extension of the spring. Plot a graph of force against extension.
- ☐ Hang a mass from the bottom of the spring and measure the new length. Calculate the extension of the spring.
- ☐ Attach a clamp to a clamp stand and hang a spring from it. Using a second clamp, secure a ruler behind the spring.
- ☐ Measure the length of the spring and record this as the original length.

When you are asked a question about a required practical, try to think back to what you did when you carried out the experiment.

Forces

Find the answer

1 Use the mark scheme to find the answer that would **not** be awarded 1 mark. Choose **A** or **B**. Explain your choice.

07.8 Define the term **inertia**. [1 mark]

Question	Answer	Mark
07.8	a measure of how difficult it is to change the velocity of an object	1

A How hard it is to change an object's velocity.

B Inertia is a measure of how hard it is to change the speed of an object. It is why seatbelts are called inertia seatbelts.

> When revising for exams, always make sure you have learned the meanings of technical terms such as **inertia**.

Answer .... would not be awarded 1 mark because ....

....

2 Use the mark scheme to find the answer that would **not** be awarded 1 mark. Choose **A, B** or **C**. Explain your choice.

04.3 What feature of a velocity–time graph can be used to determine an object's acceleration? [1 mark]

Question	Answer	Mark
04.3	the gradient	1

A Acceleration is the change in velocity over time, so if the graph is plotted with velocity on the y-axis and time on the x-axis, the gradient of the line will be equal to the object's acceleration.

B Gradient

C The area under a velocity–time graph will tell you the acceleration.

> I wish I'd known that you don't need to write answers to short-answer questions in full sentences; it would have saved me so much time in exams!

Answer .... would not be awarded 1 mark because ....

....

....

> You must learn what information the features of distance–time and velocity–time graphs can give you.

Forces

Mark the answer

1 Draw lines to connect each of the marker's comments to the relevant part of the answer.

02.1 A ball is thrown vertically upwards at a speed of 15 m/s.

Calculate the maximum height of the ball.

Assume there is no air resistance.

Give your answer to three significant figures.

$g = 9.8$ m/s² **[4 marks]**

$s = ?$

$u = 15$ m/s

$v = 0$ m/s

$a = -9.8$ m/s

$t = X$

$v^2 - u^2 = 2as$

$0^2 - 15^2 = 2 \times -9.8 \times s$

$s = 225 \div 19.6 = 11.5$ m (to 3 s.f)

Maximum height of the ball = ... 11.5 .... m

- The correct values have been substituted into the equation.
- The final velocity is correctly stated as 0 m/s at the maximum height.
- The correct equation has been selected from the Physics Equation Sheet.
- An acceleration of –9.8 m/s is correctly stated.

---

2 Now use the mark scheme below to decide how many marks you would award the answer.
Give reasons for your mark.

Question	Answer	Mark
02.1	acceleration = –9.8 m/s	1
	final velocity (v) = 0 m/s	1
	0 – 15² = (2 × –9.8 × s) (correct substitution)	1
	11.5 m	1

I would award the answer .... out of 4 marks because ....

....

....

....

Waves

Complete the answer

1 Use the hint below to complete the student's answer so that it would be awarded 2 marks.

03.7 Calculate the frequency of a wave with a time period of 12 seconds. **[2 marks]**

> **Hint**
> - Always show your working out. You may still get a mark or two, even if the final answer is incorrect.

Had a go

$T = 1 \div f$

$fT = 1$

....

....

Frequency = ... Hz

---

2 Complete the student's answer so that it would be awarded 3 marks.

04.3 A sound wave travelling in air has a frequency of 6 kHz and speed of 330 m/s.

Calculate the wavelength. **[3 marks]**

Had a go

Wave speed = frequency × wavelength

....

....

....

Wavelength = ... m

---

3 Complete the student's answer so that it would be awarded 3 marks.

03.6 Blue light has a wavelength of 4.5×10^{-7} m. The light travels a distance of 3.0 m in 1×10^{-8} s.

Calculate the frequency of blue light. **[3 marks]**

Had a go

Speed = distance ÷ time

Wave speed = frequency × wavelength

....

....

....

Frequency = ... Hz

Waves

Complete the question

1 Complete the question by adding **three** multiple-choice options. Make sure two are correct.

> 04.6 Radio waves can be reflected and refracted, just like other electromagnetic waves.
>
> Which **two** statements correctly describe features of radio waves that will undergo the most refraction in the ionosphere?
>
> Tick **two** boxes. [2 marks]
>
> Waves with a short wavelength ☐
>
> .... ✓
>
> Waves with a high frequency ☐
>
> .... ☐
>
> .... ✓

Multiple-choice answers always contain believable answers. Make sure your incorrect options really test understanding of the question.

2 Complete the question by adding **three** multiple-choice options. Make sure two are correct.

> 04.4 Which **two** of the following properties do all electromagnetic waves have in common?
>
> Tick **two** boxes. [2 marks]
>
> .... ✓
>
> They are longitudinal waves. ☐
>
> They need a medium through which to travel. ☐
>
> .... ✓
>
> .... ☐

Some students confuse the properties of waves generally and electromagnetic waves in particular. Your incorrect options could be designed to test this understanding.

Waves

Mark the answer

1 Draw lines to connect each of the marker's comments to the relevant part of the answer. One has been done for you.

07.5 A student wanted to investigate the refraction of light at an air to glass boundary. The aim of the investigation was to determine the effect of the angle of incidence on the angle of refraction.

Describe an investigation that the student could carry out in order to determine the effect.
A labelled diagram may be drawn as part of your answer. **[6 marks]**

The student should put a glass block on a piece of paper and draw around it. They should draw a normal on the piece of paper in the correct place. They should then shine a ray of light into the block and measure the angle of incidence relative to the normal. They should draw on the path of the ray as it comes out of the block and then measure the angle of refraction by joining up where it goes into and out of the block. They should measure the angles using a protractor.

- There is an explanation of which angle to measure.
- The student has given some detail about how to set up the equipment.
- The student has stated how they will measure the angles.
- The student has told the reader to mark on the path of the ray.

---

2 Now use the mark scheme below to decide how many marks you would award the answer. Give reasons for your mark

Level	Answer	Mark
3	A detailed and coherent plan covering all the steps is provided. The steps are written in a logical order and the method would lead to valid results.	5–6
2	A method is described with mostly relevant detail. The method may not be in a totally logical sequence and some detail may be missing	3–4
1	Simple statements are made. The response may lack a structure and would not lead to valid results	1–2
	No relevant content	0
	Indicative content • place a glass block on a piece of paper and draw around it • remove the block and draw a normal line at 90° to one side • use a protractor to measure the first angle of incidence • replace the glass block and with a ray box, shine a ray of light down the first line of incidence • mark where the ray emerges from the block • using a ruler, draw the refracted ray; measure the angle of refraction • repeat for a range of values of the angle of incidence	

I would award the answer .... out of 6 marks because ....
....
....
....

Re-order the answer

1 Rearrange the sentences into the most logical order by numbering each part of the answer.

01 **Figure 22** shows a diagram of a d.c. motor.

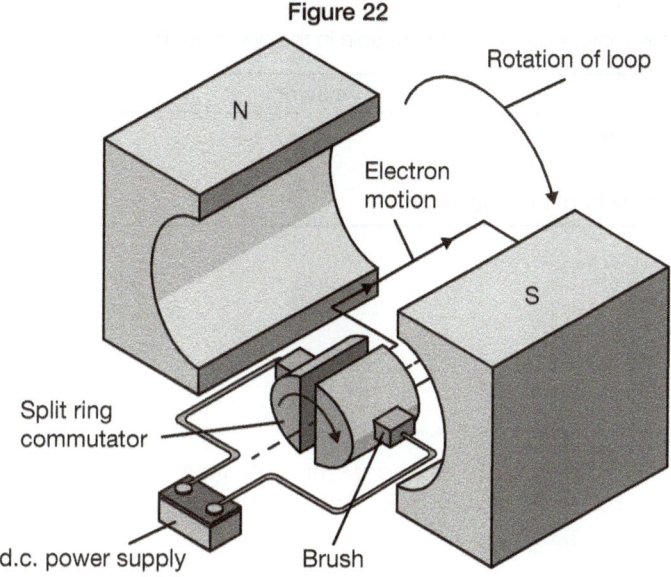

Figure 22

01.1 Explain why the coil of wire spins when the student connects the power supply. [4 marks]

☐ This creates a magnetic field around the coil of wire.

☐ A current flows in the coil of wire.

☐ The current in one side of the coil is in the opposite direction to the current in the other side of the coil, so the sides of the coil experience forces in opposite directions and the coil spins.

☐ The magnetic field from the coil interacts with the magnetic field from the permanent magnets.

Magnetism and electromagnetism

Find the answer

1 Use the mark scheme to find the answer that would **not** be awarded 1 mark. Choose **A, B** or **C**. Explain your choice.

05.7 A direct current motor can spin in either direction.

Give **one** way in which the motor could be made to spin in the opposite direction. [1 mark]

Question	Answer	Mark
05.7	reverse the current	1
	or	
	reverse the polarity of the magnets	1

A Swap the magnets.

B Reverse current.

C You could reverse the polarity of the permanent magnetic field. This would make the wire spin in the opposite direction.

Answer .... would not be awarded 1 mark because
....
....
....

2 Use the mark scheme to find the answer that would **not** be awarded 1 mark. Choose **A, B** or **C**. Explain your choice.

04.3 A student makes an electromagnet and uses it to pick up steel paper clips.

Give **one** way in which she could increase the strength of her electromagnet. [1 mark]

Question	Answer	Mark
04.3	increase the current	1
	or	
	increase the number of turns on the coil	1
	or	
	add an iron core	1

A Make the current bigger.

B Add more coils.

C Add more turns on the coil.

Answer .... would not be awarded 1 mark because
....
....
....

Magnetism and electromagnetism

Improve the answer

1 Use the hint below to write an improved answer that would be awarded 3 marks.

08.2 A wire carrying a current of 10 A passes at right angles through a magnetic field of 0.20 T.

There is a force of 0.5 N on the wire.

Calculate the length of the wire. **[3 marks]**

Had a go

Length of wire = ...25...... m

Hint
- You should always show your working out. That way, you might get a mark or two, even if your final answer is incorrect.

....
....
....

Length of wire = ... m

2 Use the hints below to write an improved answer that would be awarded 4 marks.

08.4 A wire 30 cm long passes at right angles through a magnetic field of 0.12 T.

There is a force of 0.8 N acting on the wire. Calculate the current passing through the wire. **[4 marks]**

Had a go

$F = BIl$, so $I = F \div (B \times l)$

Current = ...0.27...... A

Hints
- Once you have rearranged the equation you can substitute the values in.
- Always check the units of the quantities you are given. They must be substituted in SI units.

....
....
....

Current = ... A

Answers

Cell biology
Complete the answer

1 Use the hint below to complete the student's answer so that it would be awarded 2 marks.

03.1 Which of the cells shown in **Figure 1** is **not** an animal cell?
Give **one** reason for your answer. [2 marks]

Hint
- Think about the features of different cells. Look carefully at Figure 1 before making a decision.

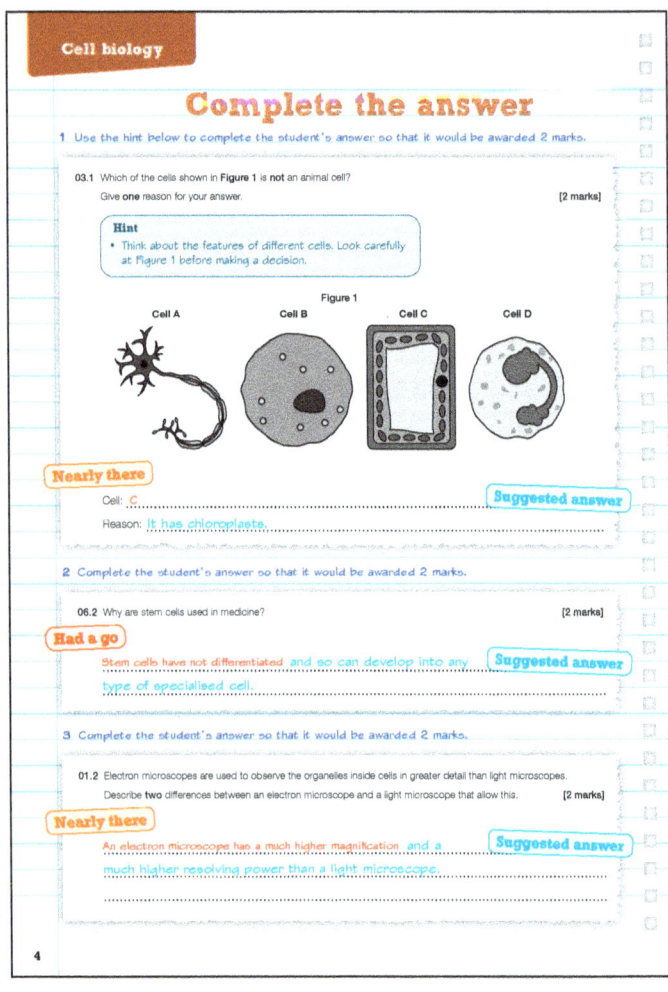

Figure 1 — Cell A, Cell B, Cell C, Cell D

Nearly there

Cell: C *Suggested answer*
Reason: It has chloroplasts.

2 Complete the student's answer so that it would be awarded 2 marks.

06.2 Why are stem cells used in medicine? [2 marks]

Had a go

Stem cells have not differentiated and so can develop into any *Suggested answer*
type of specialised cell.

3 Complete the student's answer so that it would be awarded 2 marks.

01.2 Electron microscopes are used to observe the organelles inside cells in greater detail than light microscopes.
Describe **two** differences between an electron microscope and a light microscope that allow this. [2 marks]

Nearly there

An electron microscope has a much higher magnification and a *Suggested answer*
much higher resolving power than a light microscope.

Cell biology
Complete the question

1 Complete the question by adding **two** multiple-choice options. Make sure one is correct.

03.1 Each statement below gives two structures found in cells.
Which statement gives structures that are found in **both** prokaryotic and eukaryotic cells?
Tick **one** box. [1 mark]

Suggested answer

Mitochondria and nucleus	☐
Cell membrane and cytoplasm	☑
Cell wall and mitochondria	☐
Cytoplasm and nucleus	☐

2 Complete the question by adding **two** multiple-choice options. Make sure one is correct.

04.2 Which of the following diseases can be treated using stem cells?
Tick **one** box. [1 mark]

Suggested answer

Coronary heart disease	☐
Diabetes	☑
Obesity	☐
High blood pressure	☐

Multiple-choice answers always contain believable answers. Make sure your incorrect options really test the understanding of the question.

3 Use the answer below to complete the question.

02.1 The image of a cell in a textbook is **5.2 cm** in length.
The real cell is only **130 µm**.
Calculate the magnification of the cell. [4 marks]

Magnification = size of image ÷ size of real object
5.2 cm = 52 mm
52 mm = 52 000 µm
Magnification = 52 000 ÷ 130 µm

Magnification of the cell = **× 400**

Cell biology
Mark the answer

1 Use the mark scheme below to decide how many marks you would award the answer.
Give reasons for your mark.

05.1 Active transport allows mineral ions to be absorbed into plant roots.
Explain how mineral ions are absorbed from the soil. [6 marks]

Active transport moves substances against a concentration gradient from a low concentration to a higher concentration using energy from respiration.

There are some key ideas stated. The ideas given are linked together in a logical way to give a partial explanation.

Level	Answer	Mark
3	A clear, logical explanation is provided containing accurate ideas presented in the correct order with links between ideas.	5–6
2	Key ideas of the context are presented with some ideas linked together to form a partial explanation.	3–4
1	Fragmented ideas are described. Some may be relevant with insufficient links to form an explanation. The response may explain active transport but not link it to the context.	1–2
	No relevant content	0

Indicative content
- active transport occurs when mineral ions are being moved from a low concentration to a high concentration
- the concentration of mineral ions is higher inside the root hair cell than in the soil
- mineral ions need to be taken into the cell against the concentration gradient
- carrier molecules are used to transport mineral ions across the cell membrane
- energy is required to make the carrier molecules work
- carrier molecules are specific for each substance
- the energy comes from respiration
- mineral ions are then released into the root hair cell
- this increases the concentration inside the cell

I would award the answer **2** out of 6 marks because although this is *Suggested answer*
a clear, logical explanation which covers some of the basic points, it does not
answer the question asked (i.e. how mineral ions are moved into root hair cells)
and there is no mention of carrier molecules.

Organisation
Improve the answer

1 Use the hint below to write an improved answer that would be awarded 3 marks.

03.1 Different enzymes catalyse different reactions.
Explain why enzymes are specific and only catalyse one reaction. [3 marks]

Had a go

It is like a key in a lock.

Hint
- This answer doesn't go far enough in its explanation. What is like a key in a lock and how is it like a key in a lock?

Suggested answer

The active site of the enzyme has a specific shape because of the order of the amino acids. The substrate must have a shape that fits into the active site of the enzyme. This is like a key fitting into a lock.

2 Use the hints below to write an improved answer that would be awarded 6 marks.

04.3 In plant leaves, there are different tissues that have different functions.
Explain how the structure of the tissues in a leaf is related to their functions. [6 marks]

Had a go

Some have no chloroplasts to let the light pass through. Some have lots of chloroplasts. Others are like tubes that carry water and sugar. Stomata open and closes to let water out and allow carbon dioxide in.

Hints
- This answer has identified some of the ways that tissues are differentiated but there isn't much explanation.
- This answer also uses very few scientific names for plant tissues or processes.
- Make sure you match each plant tissue with the correct function.
- You need to give a detailed description of most of the structures **and** their functions.

Suggested answer

The outer layer is the epidermis which has no chloroplasts and allows light to penetrate through to the palisade mesophyll. The palisade mesophyll has many chloroplasts near the top of the leaf to receive more light for photosynthesis. The phloem and xylem are tubes that form the transport system of the plant. Xylem carries water and minerals from the roots all over the plant, while phloem carries sugar made in the leaves to where it is needed. On the bottom of the leaf are many stomata, which can open and close to control water loss and allow carbon dioxide into the leaf.

Answers

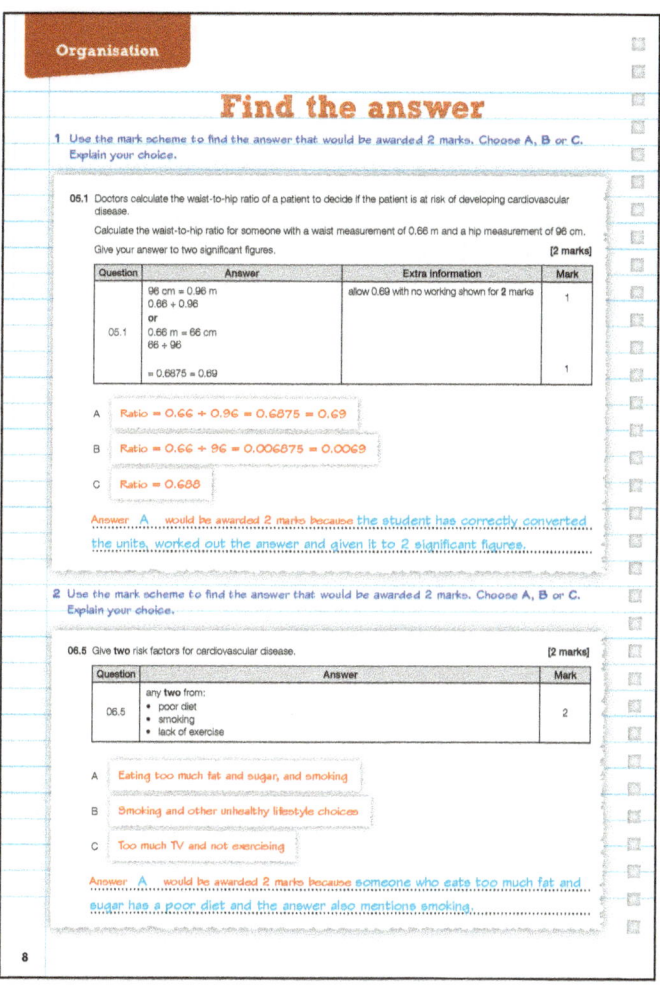

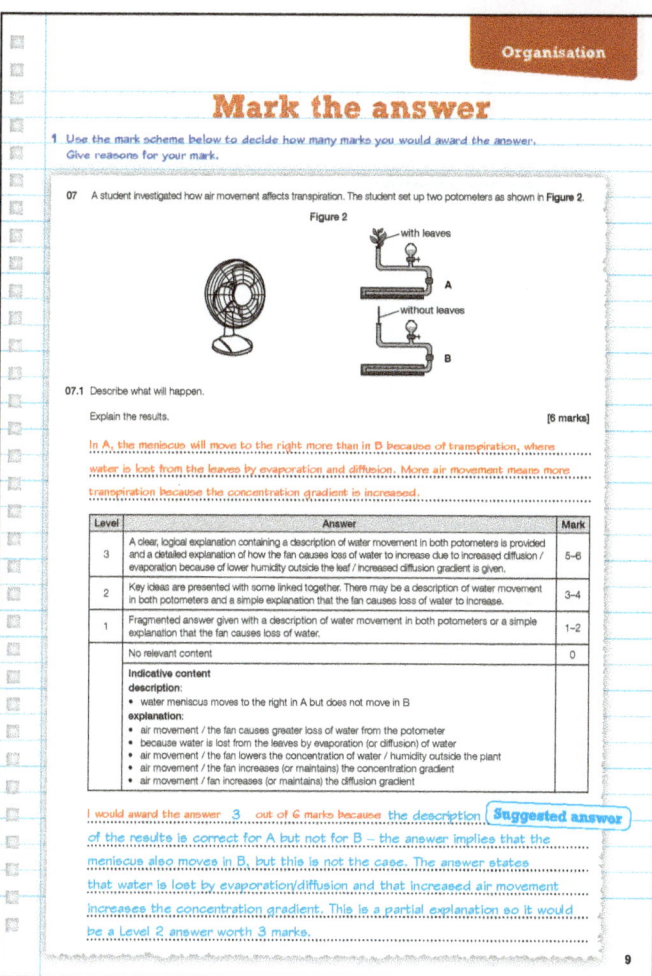

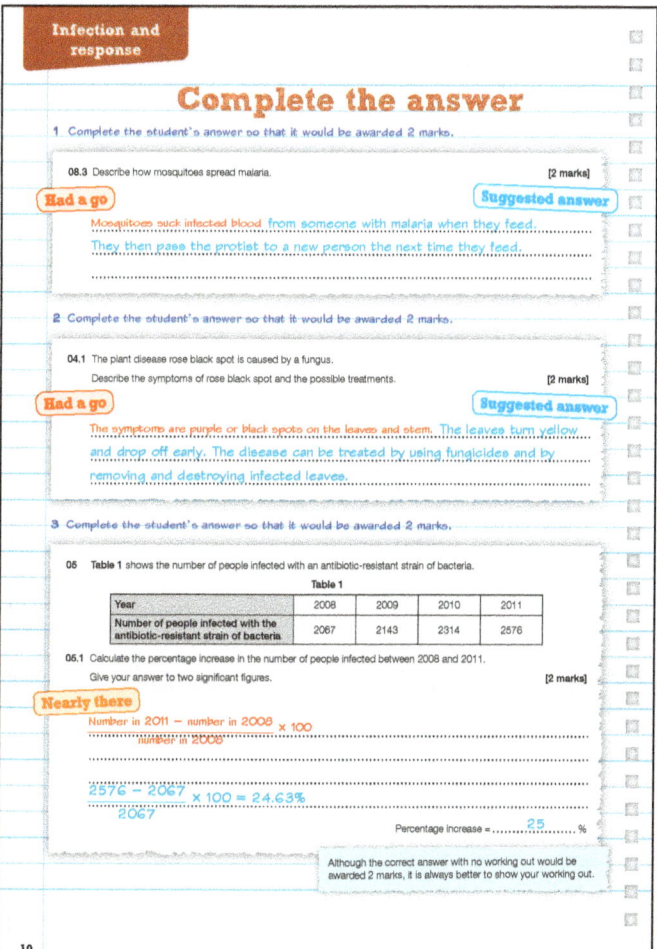

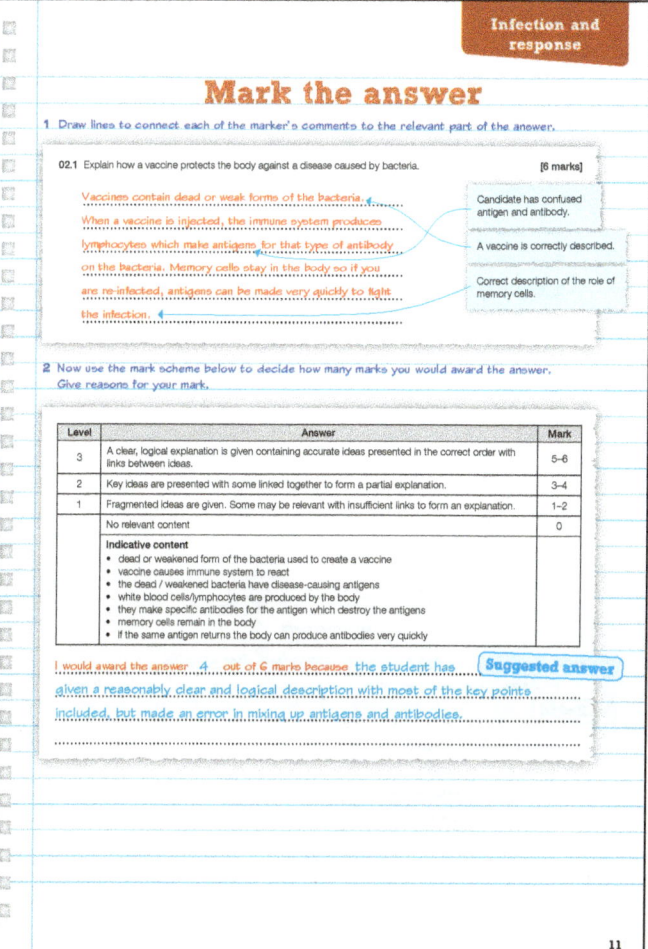

Answers

Infection and response

Complete the question

1 Complete the question by adding two multiple-choice options. Make sure one is correct.

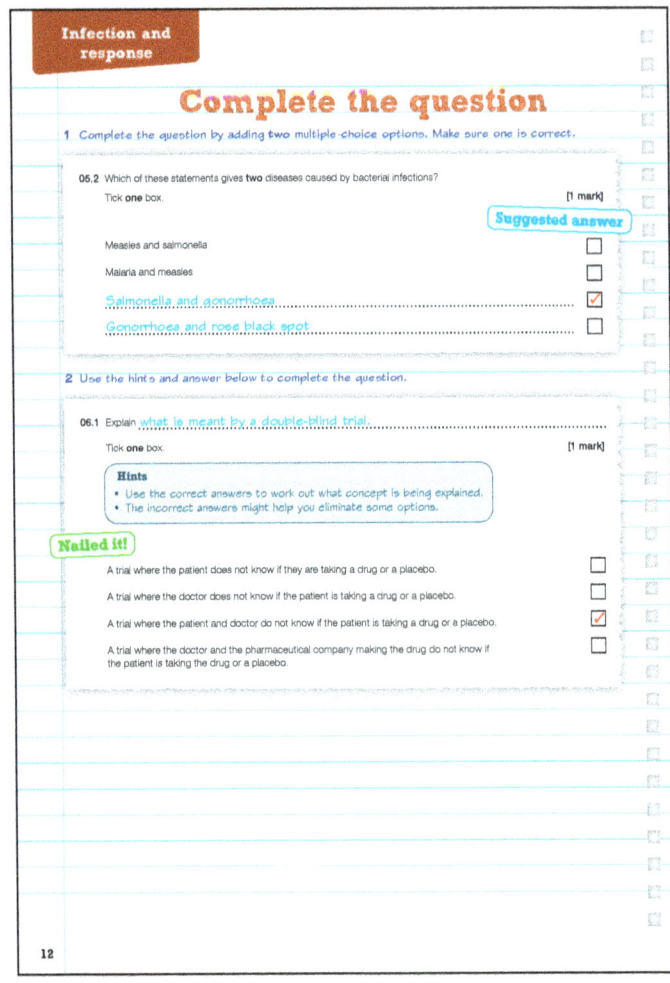

2 Use the hints and answer below to complete the question.

Nailed it!

Bioenergetics

Find the answer

1 Use the mark scheme to find the answer that would be awarded 2 marks. Choose A, B, C or D. Explain your choice.

03.1 What is the symbol equation for photosynthesis? [2 marks]

Question	Answer	Mark
03.1	correct reactants $CO_2 + H_2O$	1
	correct products $C_6H_{12}O_6 + O_2$	1

A $CO_2 + H_2O \rightarrow C_6H_{12}O_6 + CO_2$

B   water + $CO_2 \rightarrow O_2$ + energy + $C_6H_{12}O_6$

C $O_2 + H_2O \rightarrow C_6H_{12}O_6 + O_2$

D $CO_2 + H_2O \rightarrow C_6H_{12}O_6 + O_2$

Answer **D** would be awarded 2 marks because it has the correct reactants and the correct products.

2 Use the mark scheme to find the answer that would be awarded 1 mark. Choose A, B or C. Explain your choice.

04.2 Why is less energy transferred during anaerobic respiration than aerobic respiration? [1 mark]

Question	Answer	Mark
04.2	oxidation of glucose is incomplete in anaerobic respiration	1

A   Aerobic respiration produces much more energy than anaerobic respiration because the oxidation of glucose is incomplete in anaerobic respiration.

B   Aerobic respiration produces much more energy than anaerobic respiration because the oxidation of glucose is complete in anaerobic respiration.

C   Aerobic respiration produces much more energy than anaerobic respiration because the oxidation of glucose is incomplete.

Answer **A** would be awarded 1 mark because it correctly explains that the oxidation of glucose is incomplete in anaerobic respiration. Answer B is incorrect because it states that the oxidation of glucose is complete in anaerobic respiration and answer C does not specify which type of respiration it refers to.

Bioenergetics

Complete the question

1 Complete the question by adding two multiple-choice options. Make sure one is correct.

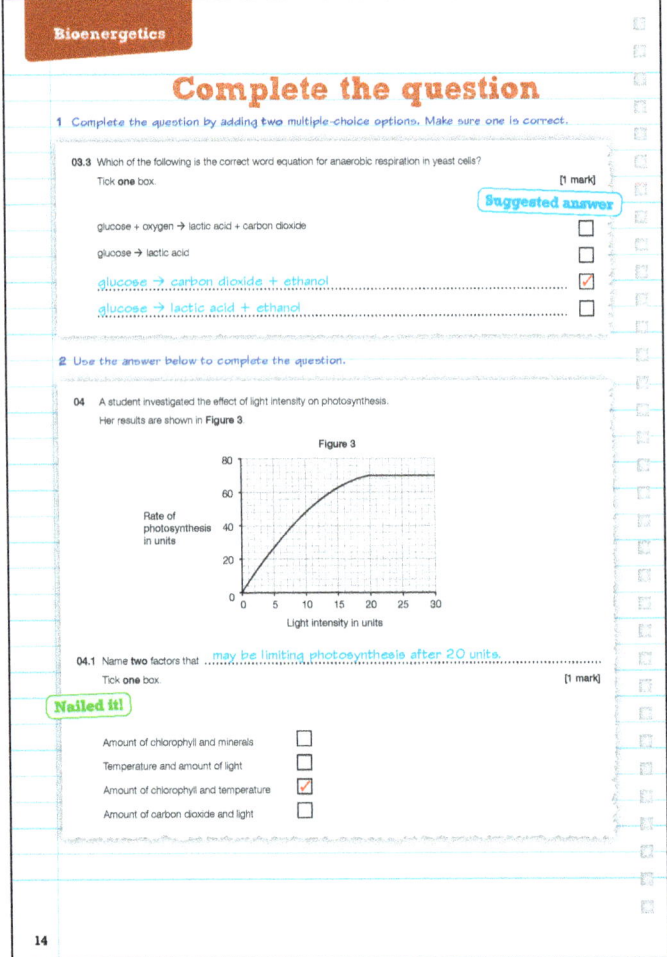

2 Use the answer below to complete the question.

Nailed it!

Bioenergetics

Re-order the answer

1 Rearrange the statements into the most logical order by numbering each part of the answer.

05.4 Describe the method used to investigate the effect of light intensity on the rate of photosynthesis. [4 marks]

2	Place the beaker containing the pondweed 10cm away from a light source.
4	Repeat the investigation with the beaker containing the pondweed 20cm, 30cm and 40cm away from the light source.
1	Take some pondweed and place it in a beaker of water in the light. Check that the pondweed is photosynthesising by looking for bubbles of oxygen being released.
3	Leave the pondweed for 5 minutes. Then use a stopwatch to count the number of bubbles produced in 1 minute by the pondweed.

When you are asked a question about a required practical, try to remember what you did when you carried out the investigation.

2 Rearrange the sentences into the most logical order by numbering each part of the answer.

06 A student is investigating the relationship between light intensity and photosynthesis.

The student measures the rate of photosynthesis for pondweed in a test tube at different distances from a light source. Light intensity is inversely proportional to the square of the distance (d) from the light source.

Light intensity = $1 \div d^2$

06.1 Suggest how the student could analyse the relationship between light intensity and the rate of photosynthesis. Use the equation in your answer. [4 marks]

1	Square the distance between the lamp and the plant.
3	Plot a graph of the rate of photosynthesis against $1 \div d^2$.
4	The graph should show that the rate of photosynthesis increases with light intensity.
2	Calculate the inverse of the distance from the lamp to the plant.

78

Answers

Bioenergetics

Improve the answer

1 Use the hint below to write an improved answer that would be awarded 4 marks.

> **07.1** Pine trees often grow on exposed hillsides.
> The cooler temperatures, windy conditions and dry soil affect the growth of the trees.
> How would this affect the growth of trees? Explain why. [4 marks]

Had a go
Lower temperatures and high winds decrease the rate of photosynthesis.

Hint
- The student has correctly identified the factors affecting growth but hasn't explained how and why these factors have affected it.

Suggested answer
Lower temperatures decrease the rate of photosynthesis because the enzymes in the cells work more slowly as they are not at their optimum temperature. There are also fewer collisions between enzyme and substrate molecules at lower temperatures, so the rate of reaction decreases. High winds decrease the rate of photosynthesis because the stomata close so less carbon dioxide is taken into the leaf. Glucose produced by photosynthesis is needed to make proteins for growth, so the lower rate of photosynthesis slows down the growth of trees.

2 Write an improved answer that would be awarded 4 marks.

> **08.1** The apparatus shown in **Figure 4** can be used to measure respiration in peas.
> Describe the results you would expect. Explain why. [4 marks]

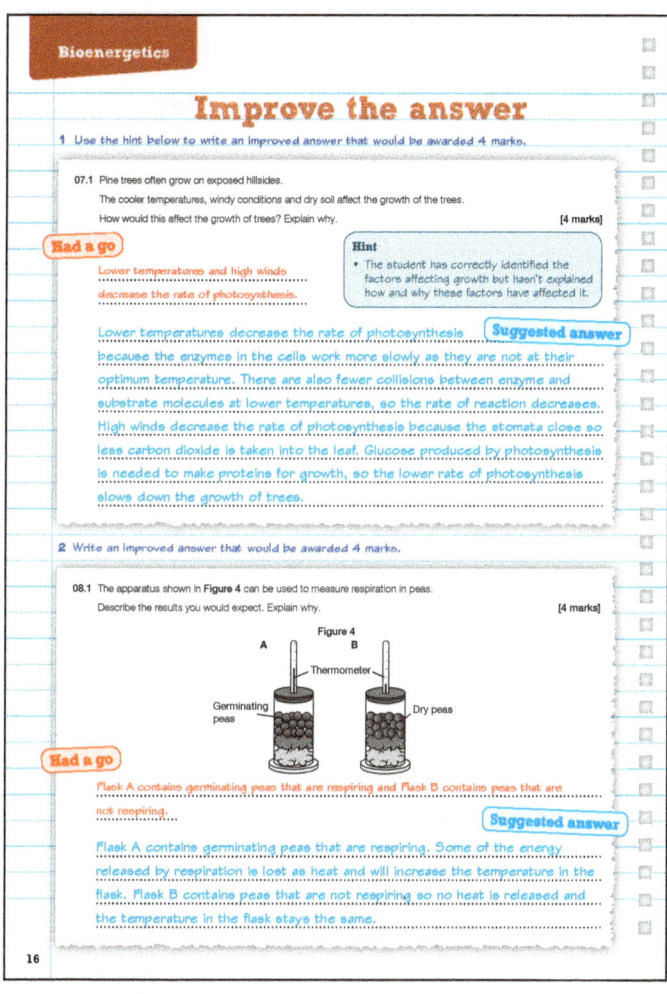

Figure 4

Had a go
Flask A contains germinating peas that are respiring and Flask B contains peas that are not respiring.

Suggested answer
Flask A contains germinating peas that are respiring. Some of the energy released by respiration is lost as heat and will increase the temperature in the flask. Flask B contains peas that are not respiring so no heat is released and the temperature in the flask stays the same.

Homeostasis and response

Mark the answer

1 Draw lines to connect each of the marker's comments to the relevant part of the answer.

> **01.4** Explain how glucagon interacts with insulin to control blood sugar. [6 marks]

Insulin and glucagon balance blood sugar levels using negative feedback. When blood glucose is too high after a meal, insulin in the blood makes the liver convert glucose to glycogen to store it and lower the blood sugar level. If blood sugar is too low, insulin production stops and glucagon in the blood makes the liver change the glycogen into glucose to increase blood glucose. No more glucagon is then produced.

- Correct description of the role of the liver.
- No mention of the role of the pancreas in monitoring blood glucose and secreting insulin.
- The explanation is constructed well in a step-by-step way. It follows the negative feedback cycle clearly, starting with what happens when blood sugar is too high and then explaining what happens when blood sugar levels are too low.

2 Now use the mark scheme below to decide how many marks you would award the answer. Give reasons for your mark.

Level	Answer	Mark
3	A clear, logical explanation is given containing accurate ideas presented in the correct order with links made between ideas.	5–6
2	Key ideas are presented with some linked together to form a partial explanation.	3–4
1	Fragmented ideas are presented. Some may be relevant, with insufficient links to form an explanation.	1–2
	No relevant content.	0

Indicative content
- cells in pancreas detect/monitor blood glucose concentration
- if blood glucose concentration is too high, the pancreas secretes insulin into blood
- at the liver/target organ, blood glucose is absorbed and converted into glycogen for storage
- if blood glucose level is too low, pancreas secretes glucagon into blood
- at the liver/target organ, glycogen is converted into glucose and released into the blood
- this is a negative feedback cycle

Suggested answer
I would award the answer **5** out of 6 marks because this is a comprehensive attempt to answer the question. Most key ideas are stated and have been clearly linked to form a good explanation. It does not score 6 marks as there is no mention of the role of the pancreas in the negative feedback cycle.

Homeostasis and response

Complete the answer

1 Complete the student's answer so that it would be awarded 2 marks.

> **11.2** There are two types of diabetes.
> Explain how Type 1 diabetes differs from Type 2 diabetes. [2 marks]

Type 1 diabetes happens due to the pancreas not producing enough insulin so blood sugar levels are very high.
It can be treated by insulin injections. Type 2 diabetes happens due to body cells not responding to insulin produced by the pancreas.
It can be treated by a carbohydrate-controlled diet and exercise.

2 Complete the student's answer so that it would be awarded 3 marks.

> **07.2** Explain how the endocrine system works to control and co-ordinate the body. [3 marks]

The endocrine system consists of a number of glands in the body.
Hormones are secreted by the glands into the bloodstream.
Hormones work on target organs to produce an effect.

3 Complete the student's answer so that it would be awarded 4 marks.

> **04.3** In vitro fertilisation (IVF) is used to treat infertility.
> Explain the advantages and disadvantages of IVF. [4 marks]

The benefit of using IVF is that it can enable women with fertility problems to have their own child.
However, the disadvantages of using IVF are that the success rates are not high and using FSH and LH can cause multiple births.
This is emotionally and physically very stressful for both parents.

Suggested answer

Homeostasis and response

Complete the question

1 Complete the question by adding two multiple-choice options. Make sure one is correct.

> **06.2** Why is homeostasis important in living things?
> Tick **one** box. [1 mark]

Suggested answer

It ensures that enzymes have the optimum conditions.	☒
It increases the amount of blood glucose.	☐
It ensures that cells have sufficient oxygen for respiration.	☐
It makes sure that reaction times in animals are very fast.	☐

2 Use the answer below to complete the question.

> **05.3** Negative feedback systems control hormone levels in the blood.
> Explain how thyroxine levels are controlled by negative feedback. [2 marks]

Nailed it!
The hypothalamus detects a drop in internal body temperature and low levels of thyroxine in the blood. This triggers the hypothalamus to send a message to the pituitary gland to release TSH. Increased levels of TSH cause the thyroid gland to produce thyroxine. Thyroxine increases metabolic rate. When higher thyroxine levels are detected by the hypothalamus and pituitary gland, they inhibit the release of TSH and thyroxine levels in the blood drop.

3 Use the multiple-choice options below to complete the question.

> **03.2** Which hormones are responsible for the maturation and release of an egg? [1 mark]

Nailed it!

Oestrogen and follicle-stimulating hormone	☐
Oestrogen and luteinising hormone	☐
Luteinising hormone and progesterone	☐
Follicle-stimulating hormone and luteinising hormone	☒

79

Answers

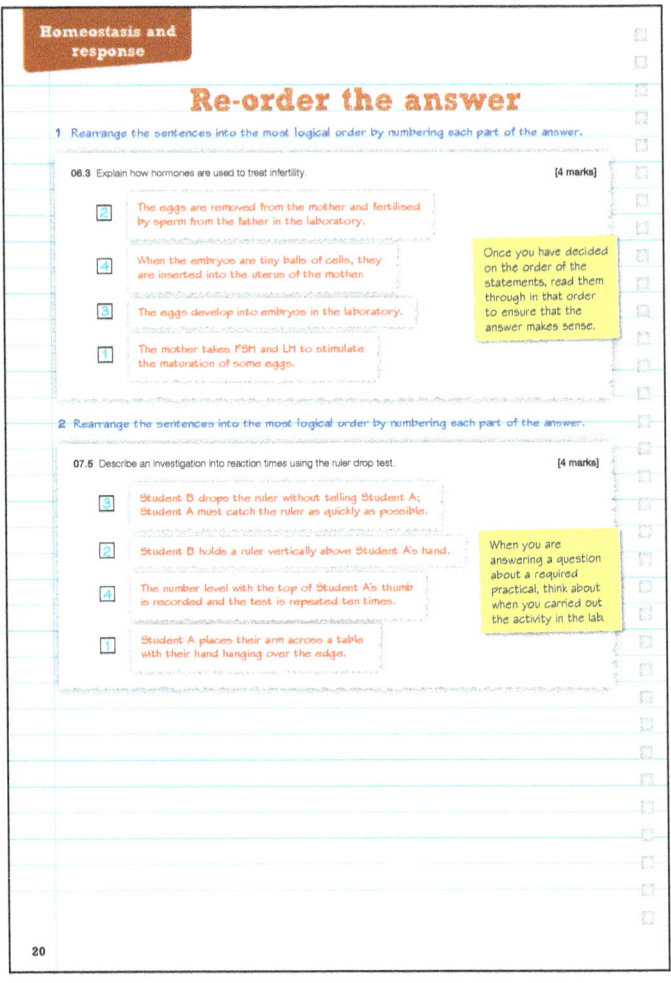

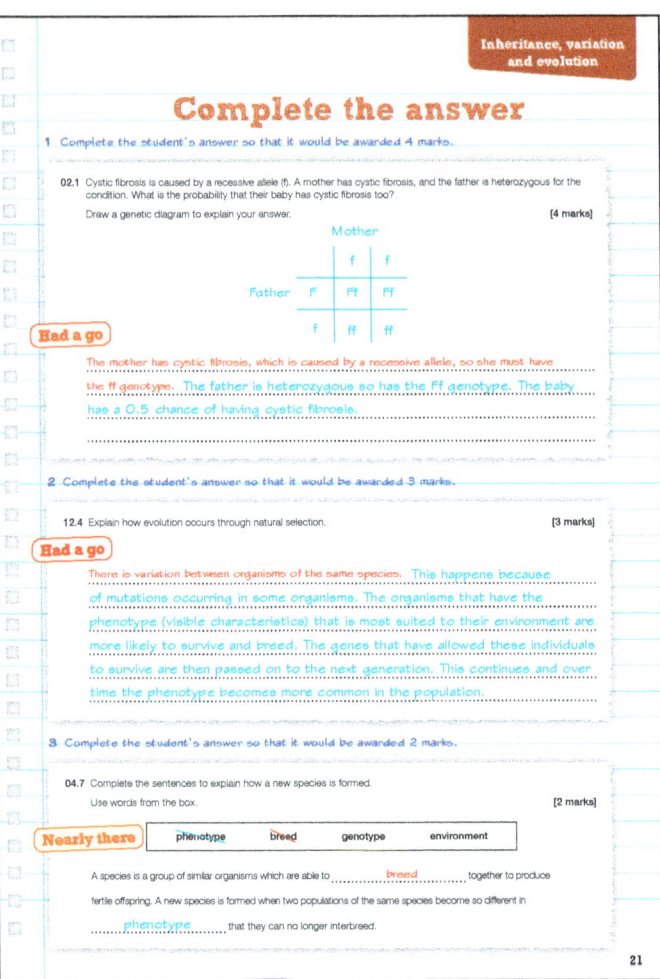

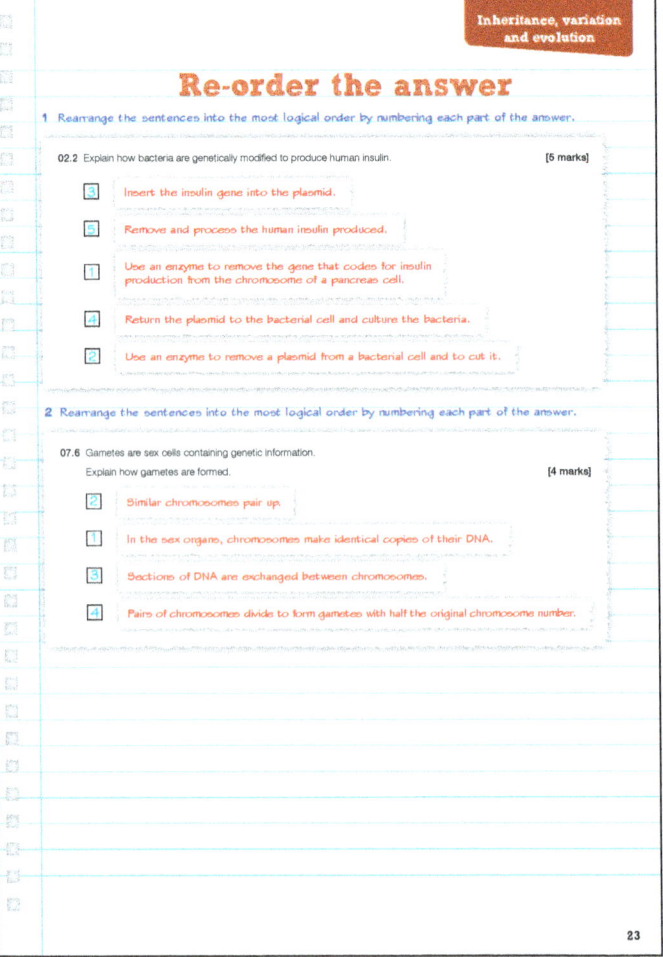

Answers

Ecology

Complete the question

1. Use the student's answer below to complete the question.

Suggested answer

12.1 All species live in ecosystems. They consist of communities of plants and animals that are adapted to the abiotic and biotic conditions of that ecosystem.

Name **three abiotic factors that affect plants growing in a field.** [1 mark]

Nailed it!

Temperature, light intensity, carbon dioxide levels

The answer lists three things so you know that the question must have asked for three factors.

2. Complete the question by adding two multiple-choice options. Make sure one is correct.

Suggested answer

07.1 Which **one** of the following may cause water pollution?
Tick **one** box. [1 mark]

- Smoke ☐
- Landfill ☐
- Fertiliser ☑
- Algae ☐

3. Complete the question by adding two multiple-choice options. Make sure one is correct.

Suggested answer

08.4 Which of the following is a reason for the large-scale deforestation happening in some countries?
Tick **one** box. [1 mark]

- To reduce CO_2 levels ☐
- For new landfill sites ☐
- To grow biofuels ☑
- To provide new habitats to increase biodiversity ☐

Ecology

Re-order the answer

1. Rearrange the sentences into the most logical order by numbering each part of the answer. One has been done for you.

04.4 Describe the main stages of the carbon cycle. [5 marks]

[4] Animals and plants die and are eaten by decomposers. The carbon in the dead organisms is released back into the atmosphere as carbon dioxide.

[3] Consumers feed on plants, passing the carbon in them up the food chain.

[2] Producers use carbon dioxide in the atmosphere to photosynthesise and make carbohydrates.

[1] When animals and plants respire, and fuels are burned, carbon is released into the atmosphere.

[5] If dead animals and plants cannot decompose, fossil fuels containing carbon may be formed.

2. Rearrange the sentences into the most logical order by numbering each part of the answer.

05.1 Some animal populations are dependent on each other. Lions are predators that feed on gazelles.
Explain how the lion population affects the gazelle population. [2 marks]

[1] Lions eat gazelles and the gazelle population falls.

[4] There is plenty of food for lions to feed and reproduce, so their population increases.

[2] There is insufficient food to maintain the lion population so the lion population falls.

[3] Fewer lions are feeding on gazelles, so the gazelle population starts to increase.

Ecology

Mark the answer

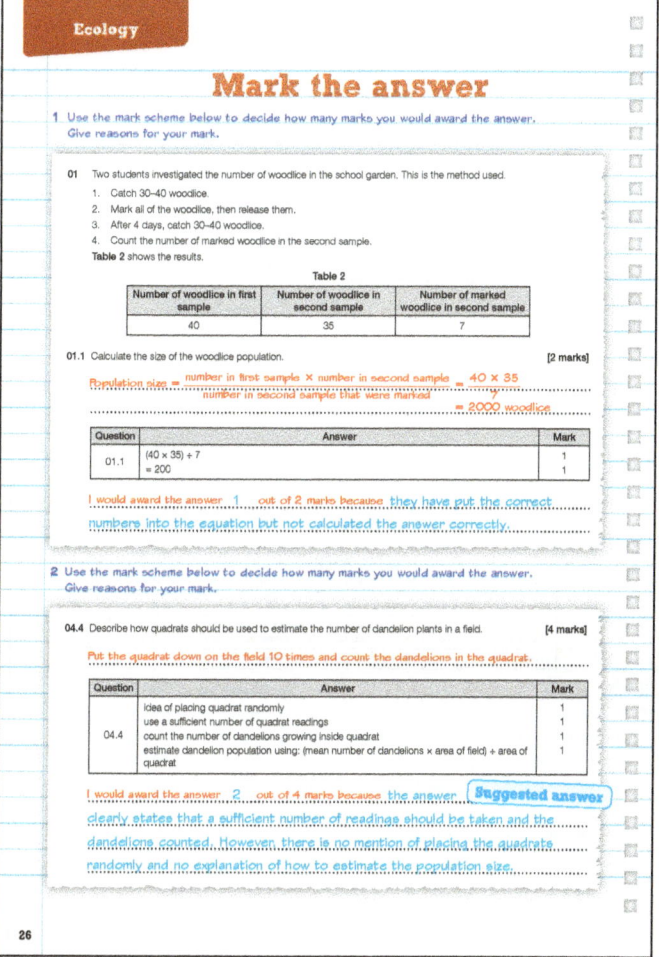

Ecology

Complete the answer

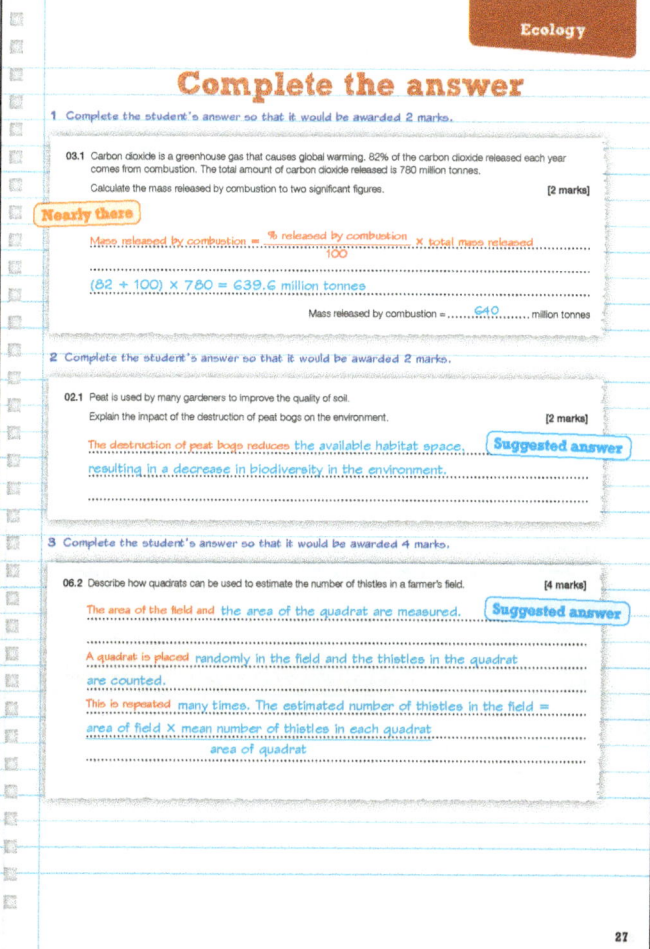

Answers

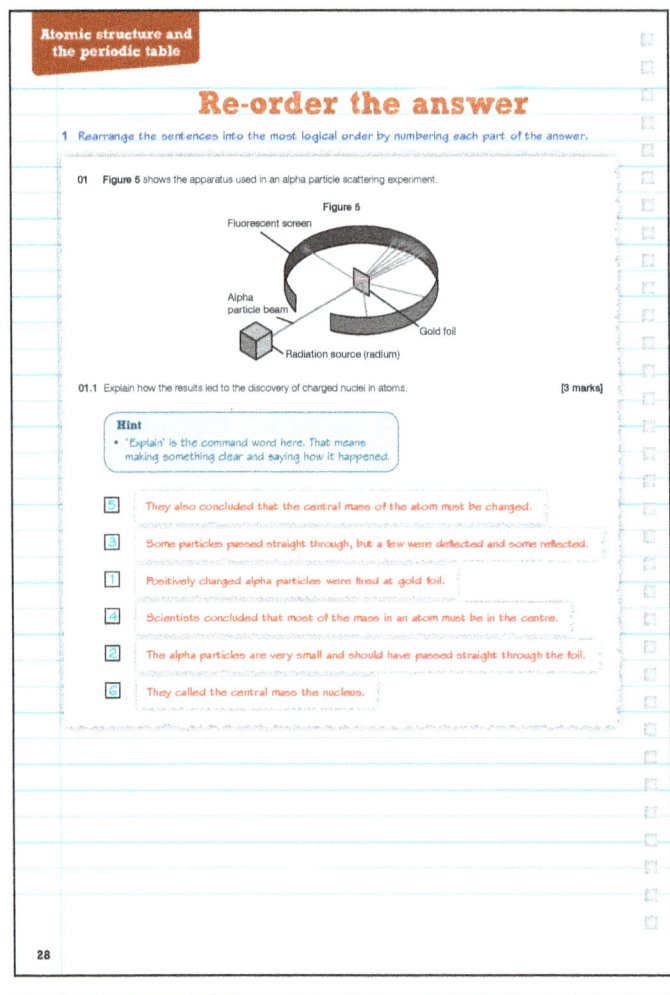

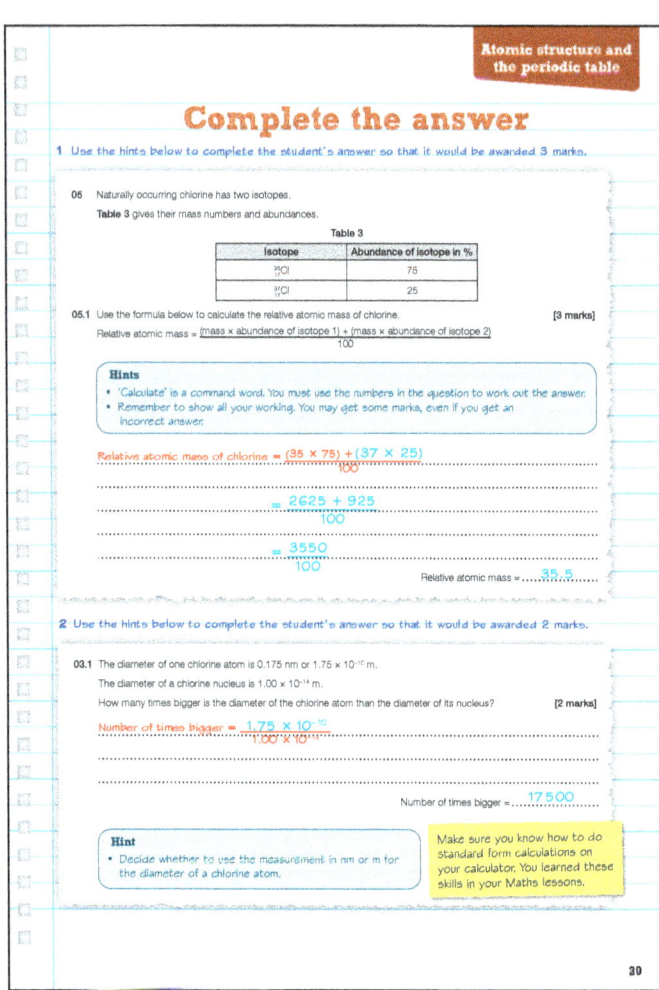

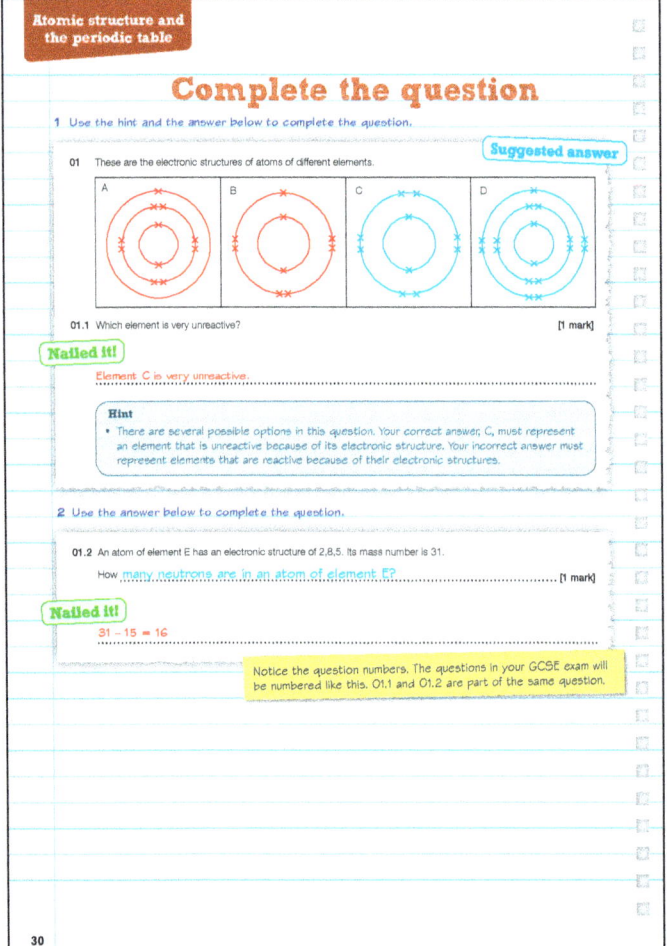

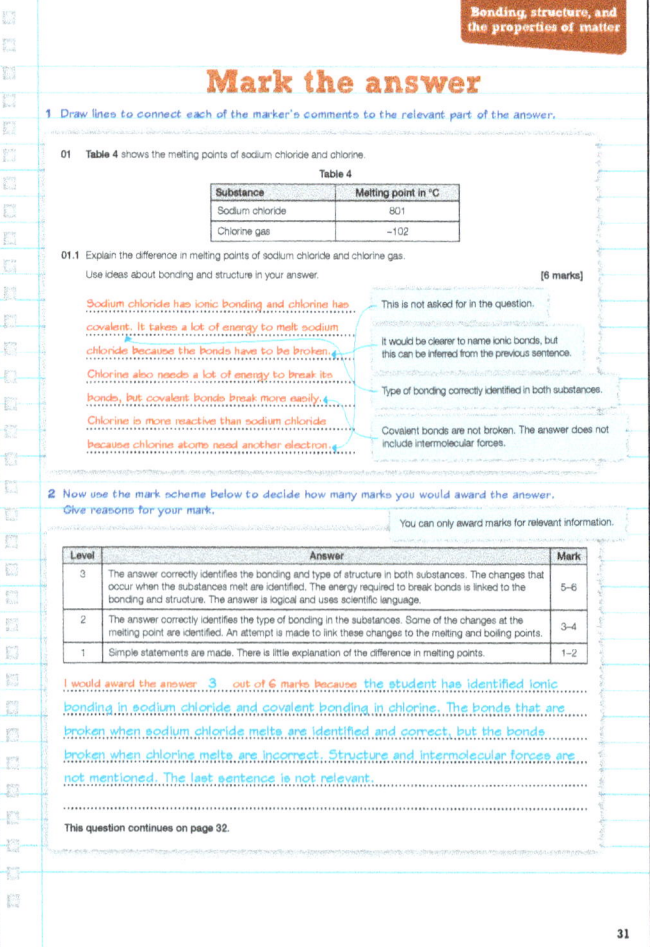

Answers

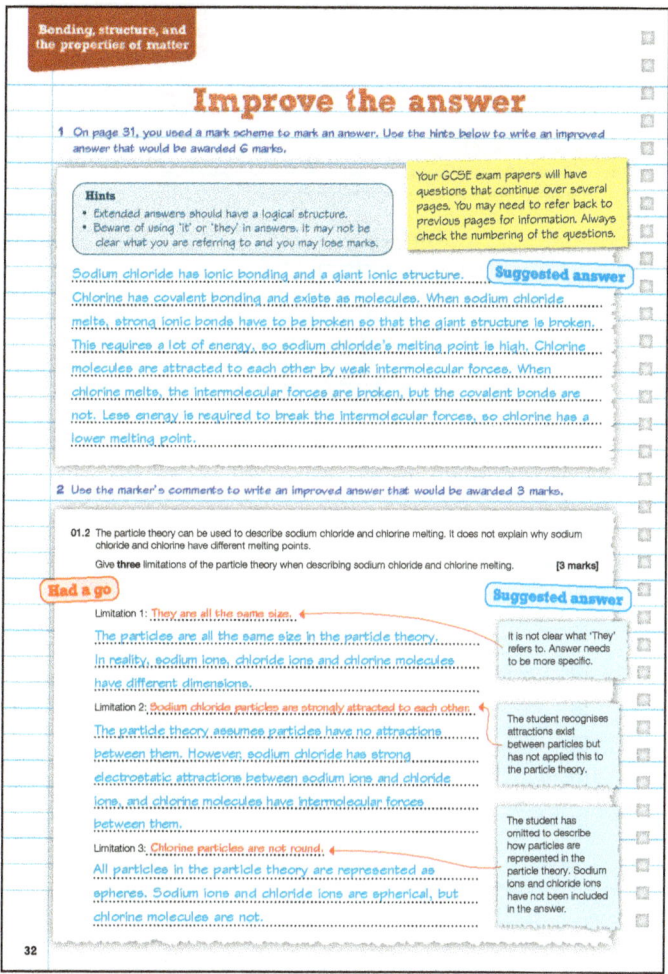

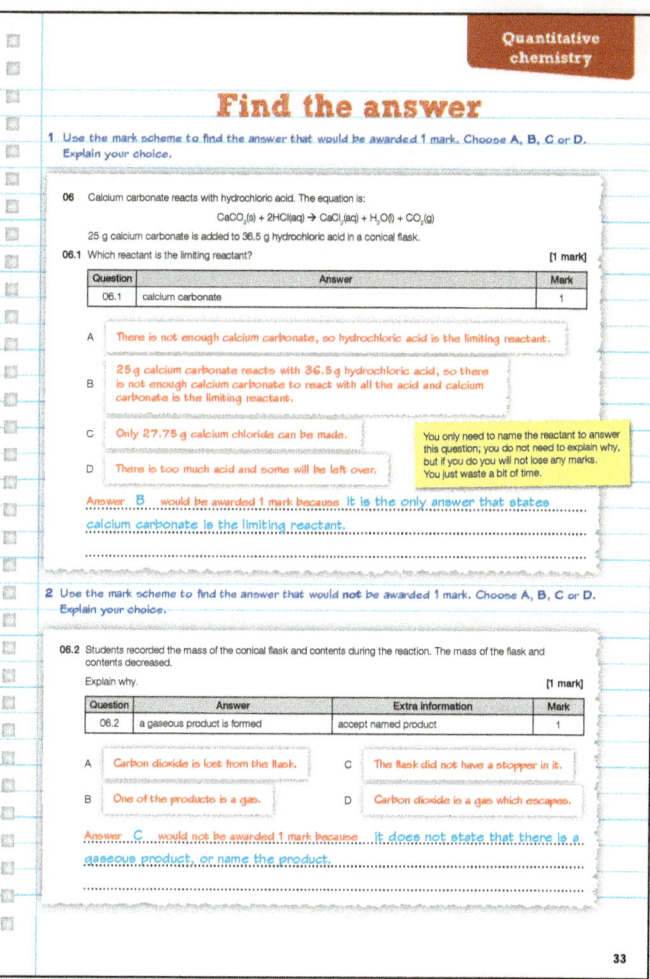

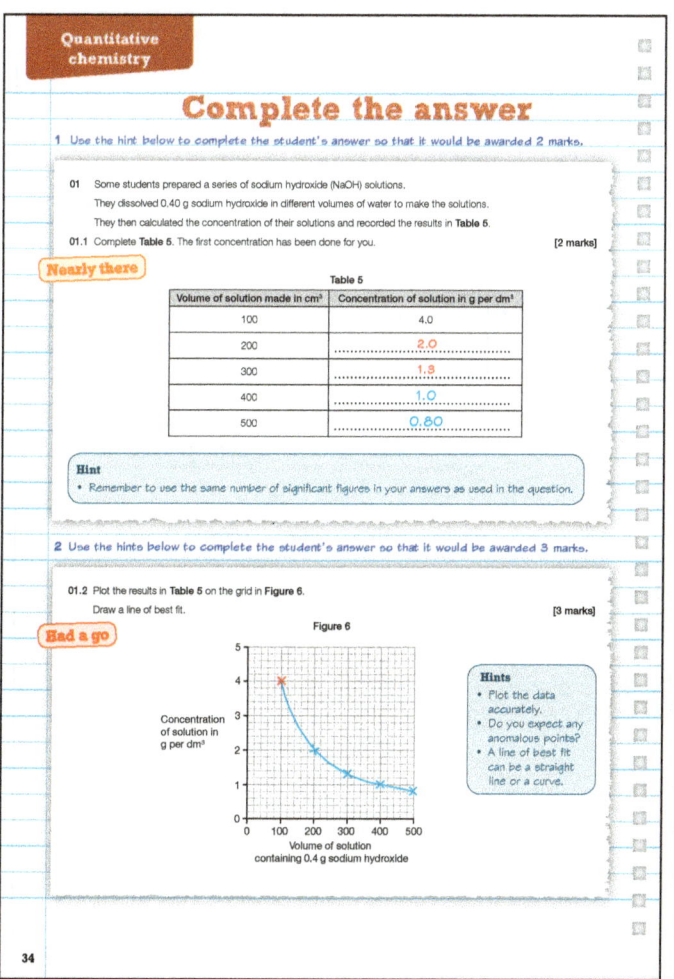

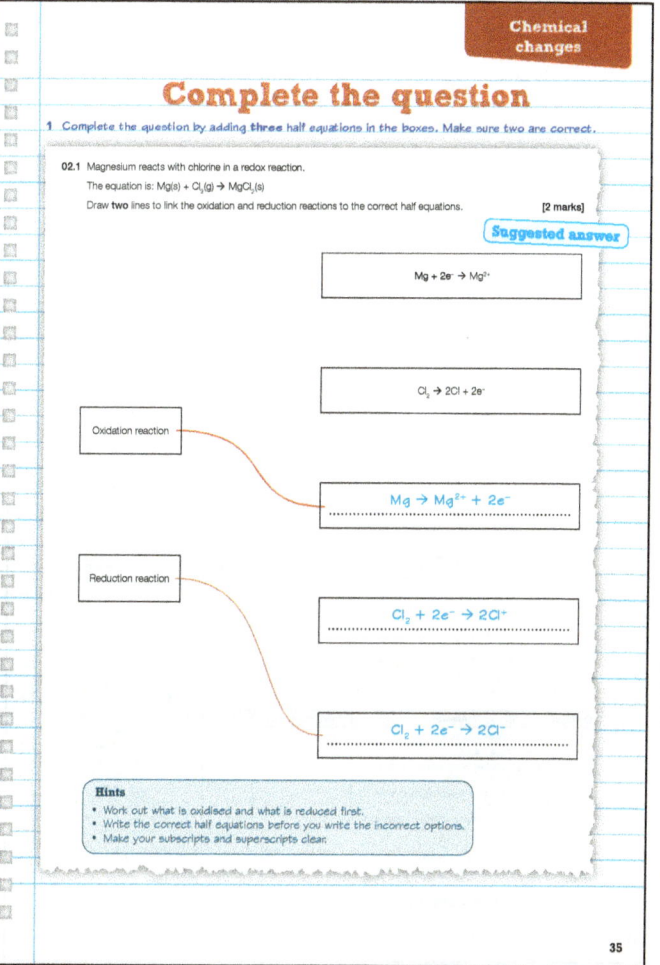

Answers

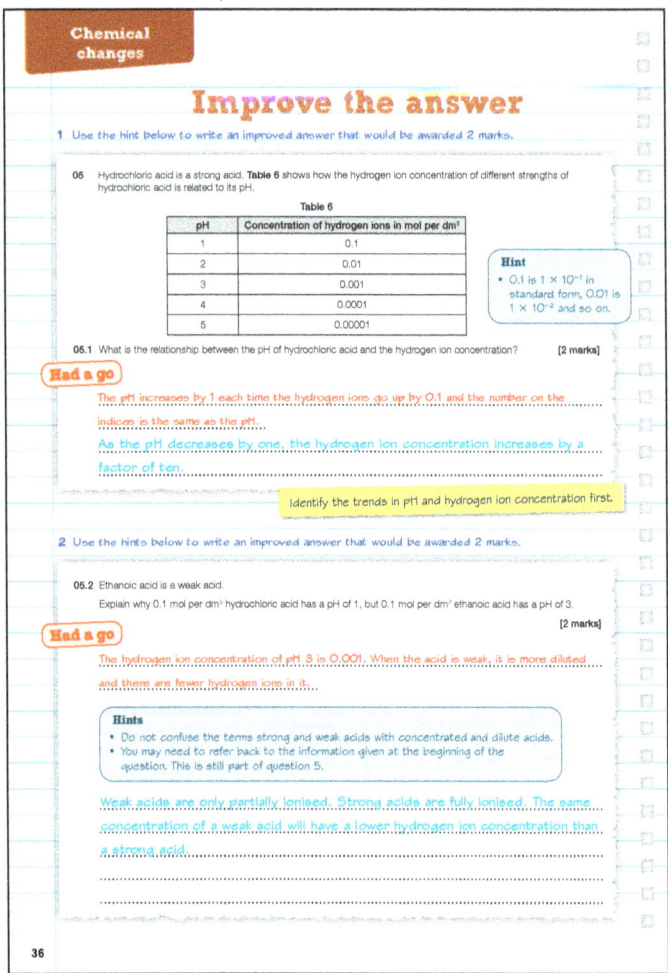

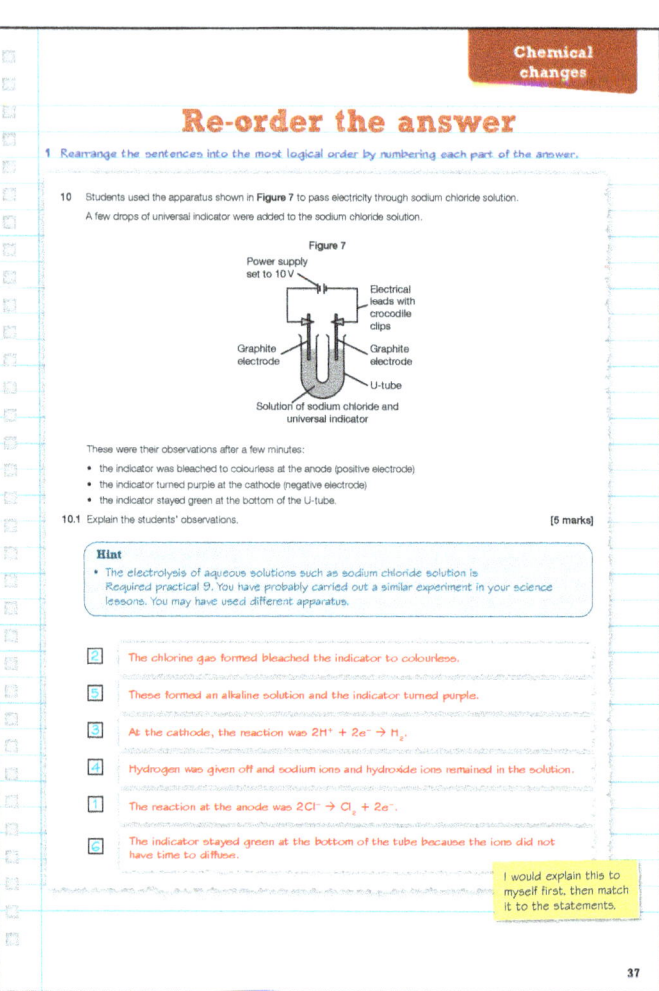

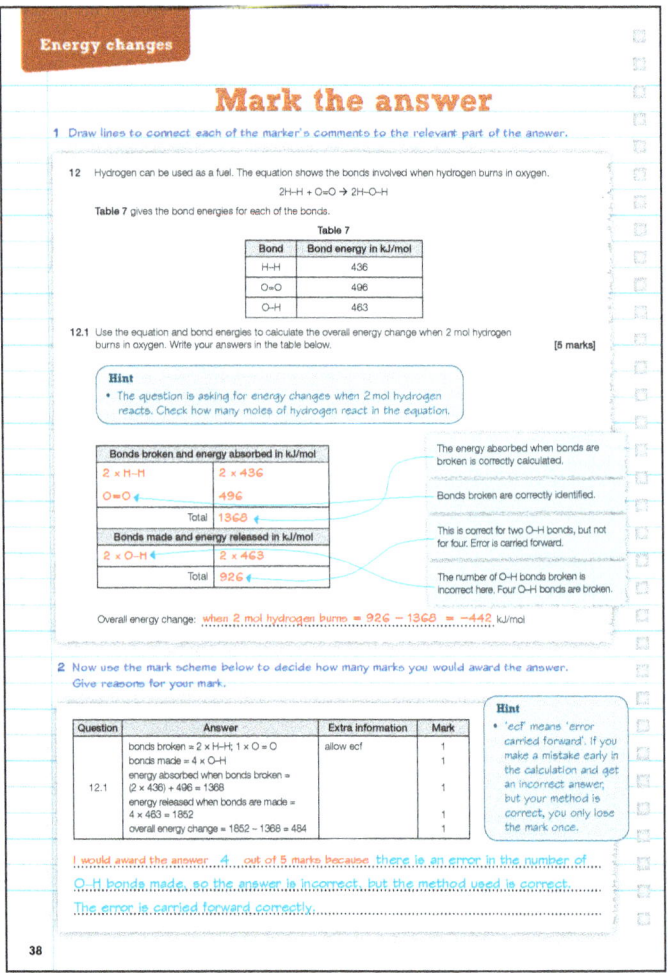

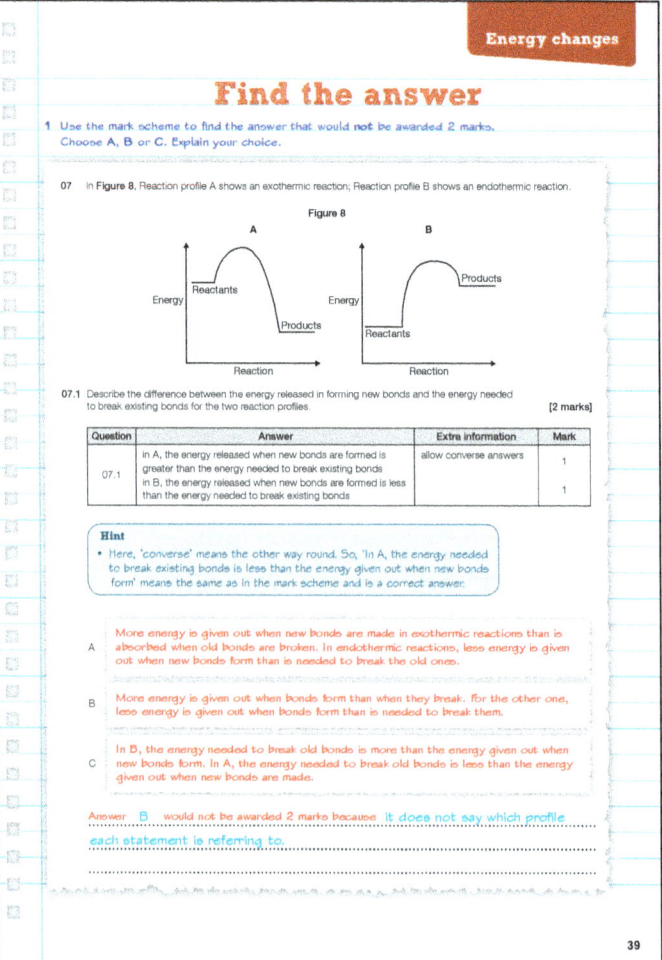

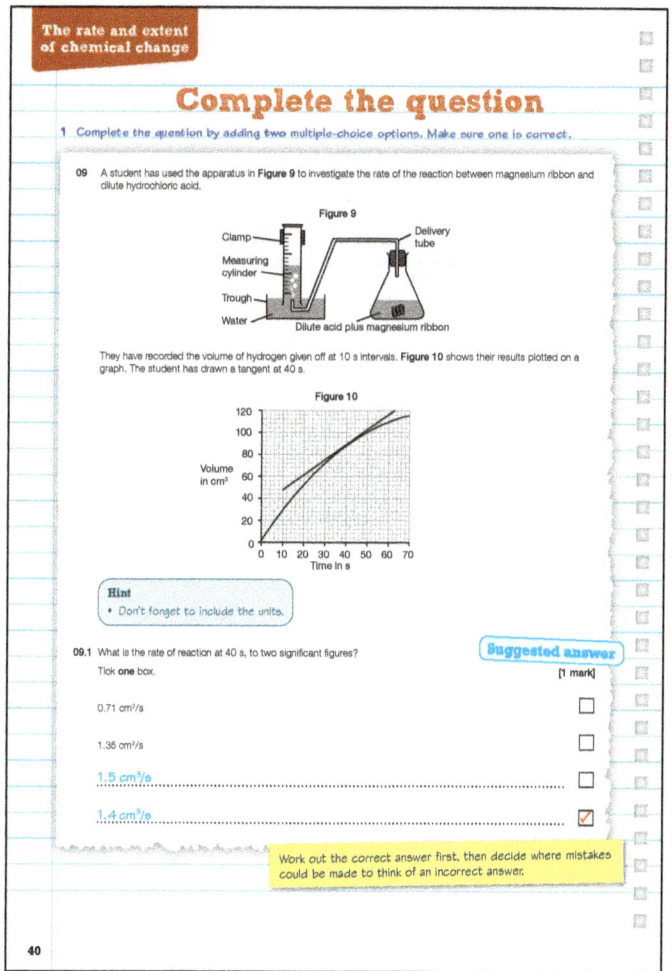
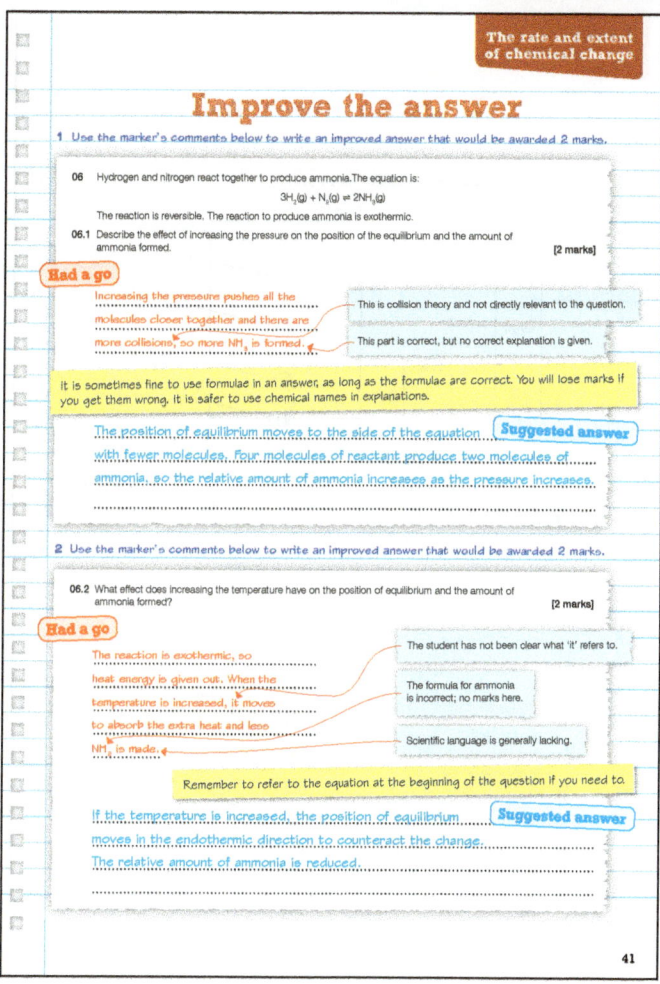
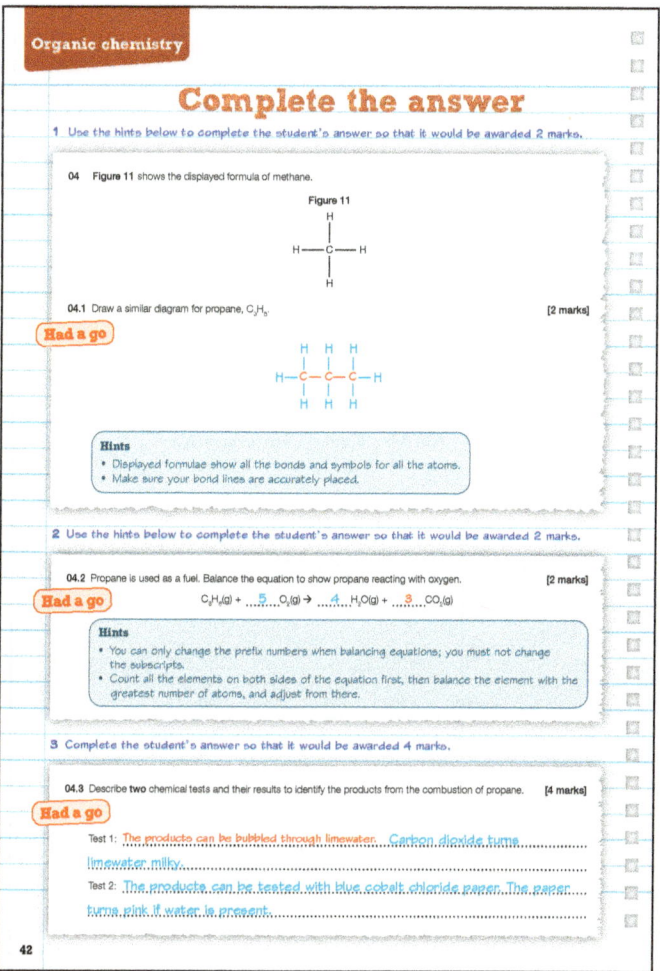
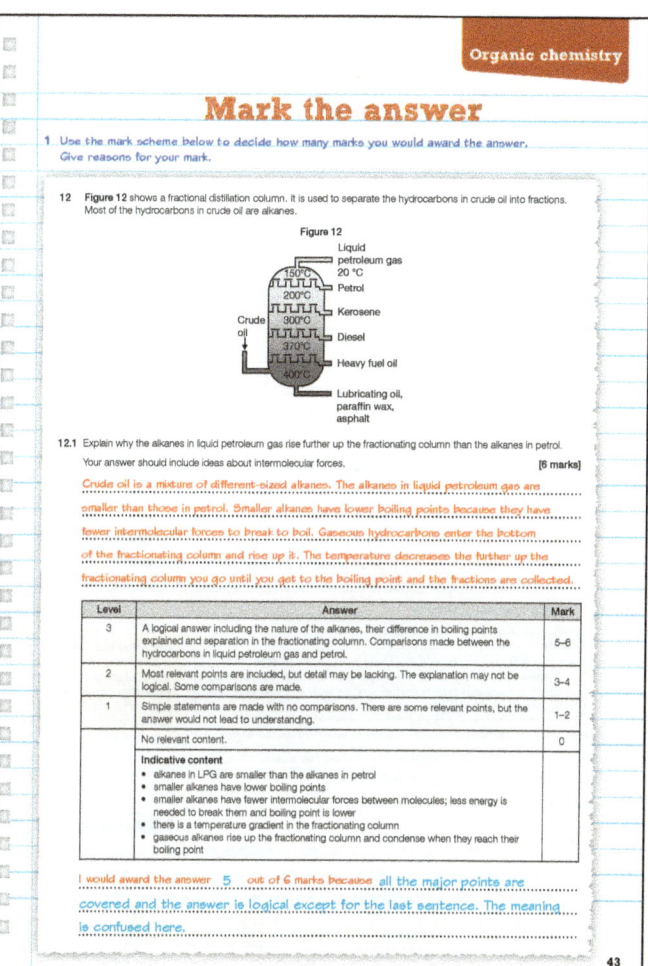

Answers

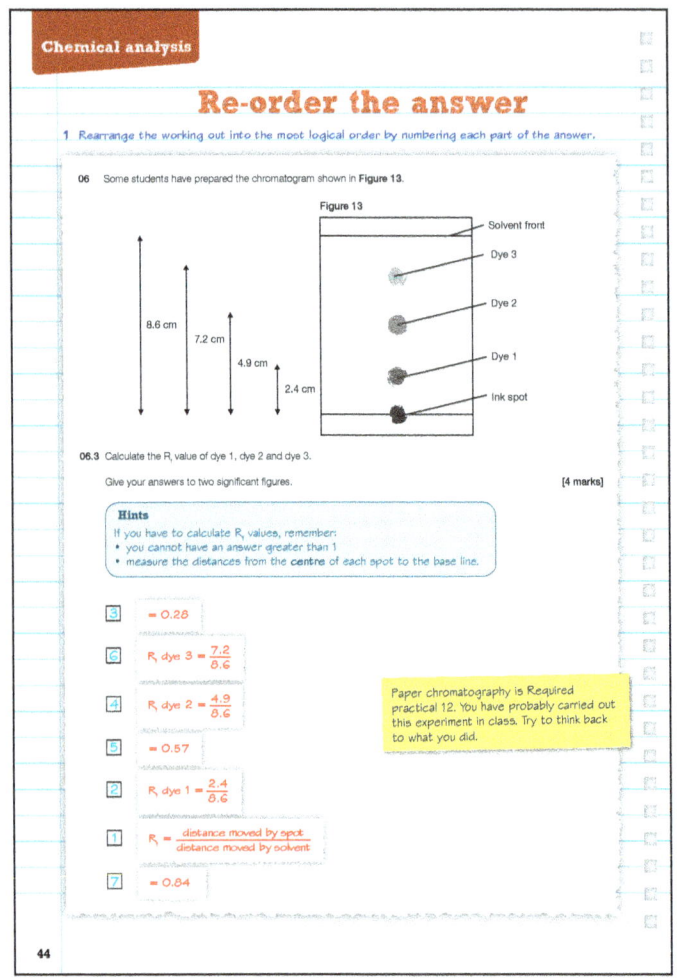

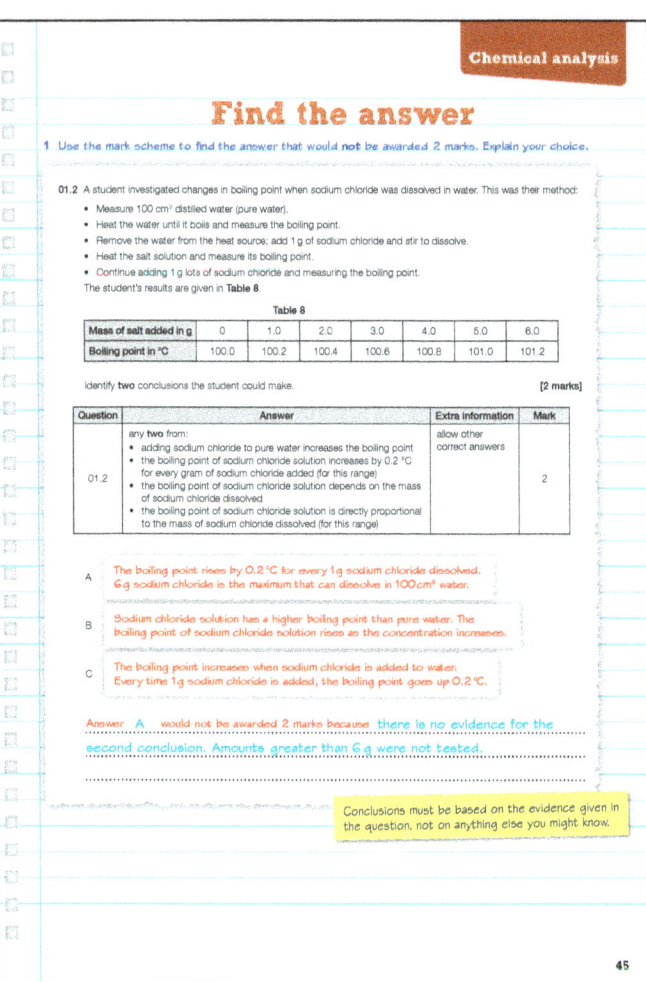

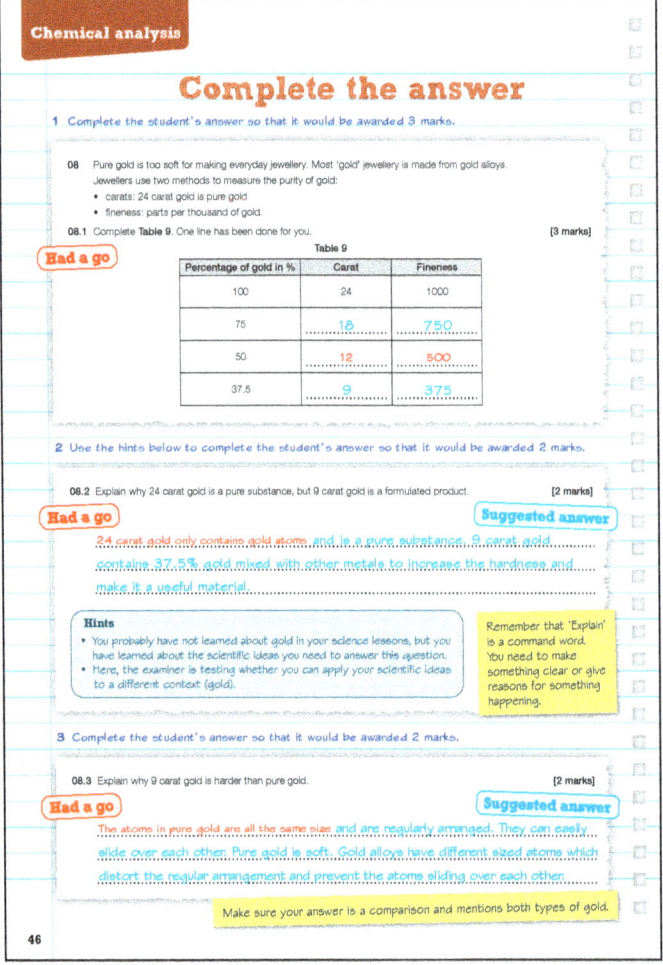

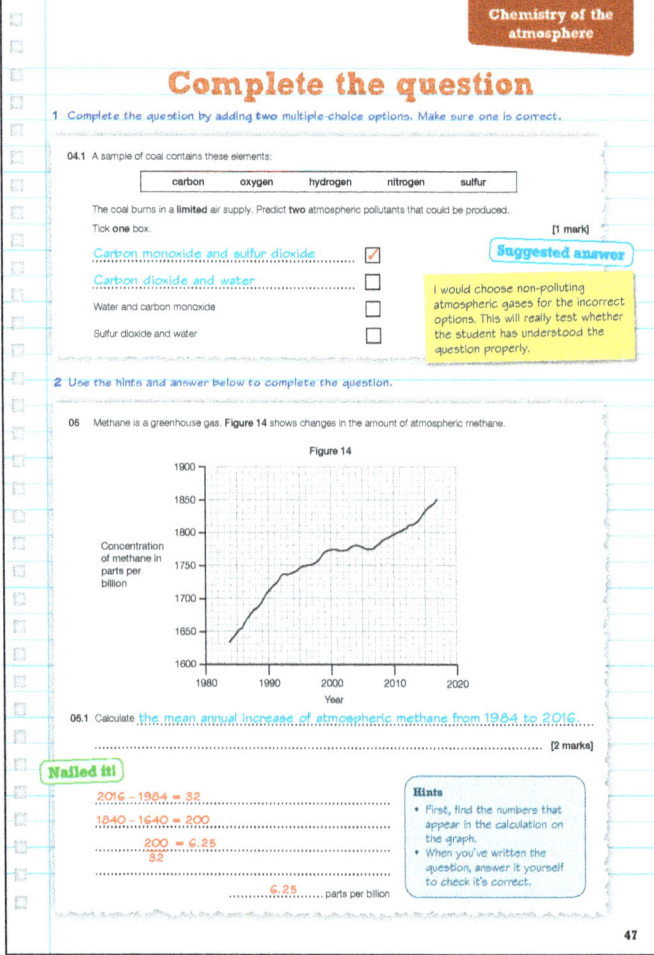

Chemistry of the atmosphere

Find the answer

1 Use the mark scheme to find the answer that would **not** be awarded 2 marks. Choose A, B, C or D. Explain your choice.

07 The carbon footprint of one pair of jeans is calculated to be 33.44 kg carbon dioxide and other greenhouse gases.

This includes the following contributors:

- growing and harvesting the cotton
- producing the denim fabric
- manufacturing the jeans
- all transport and energy
- use of the jeans (washing etc.)
- disposal of the jeans

07.1 Identify **two** ways in which the carbon footprint can be reduced. **[2 marks]**

Question	Answer	Extra information	Mark
07.1	any **two** from: • strategies to use alternative energy sources • energy saving strategies • strategies to reduce transport • washing less frequently • recycling	allow specific answers allow other correct answers	2

A Use solar power to provide the electricity and wear the jeans for longer before washing them.

B Use natural gas instead of coal or oil to provide the energy. Natural gas does not produce carbon dioxide when burned.

C Manufacture the jeans where the cotton is grown and use hydroelectric power to provide the energy.

D Wash the jeans at a lower temperature and send them to a charity shop when you have finished with them.

Read all the answers before deciding which one would **not** get 2 marks.

Answer B would not be awarded 2 marks because natural gas is mostly methane which contains carbon. This produces carbon dioxide when it is used as a fuel. The student has not understood why natural gas is less polluting than coal or oil and has only given one reason.

Hints
- Remember that the carbon footprint involves the full life cycle of a product.
- There are many correct answers to this question. The mark scheme only gives a few.

48

Chemistry of the atmosphere

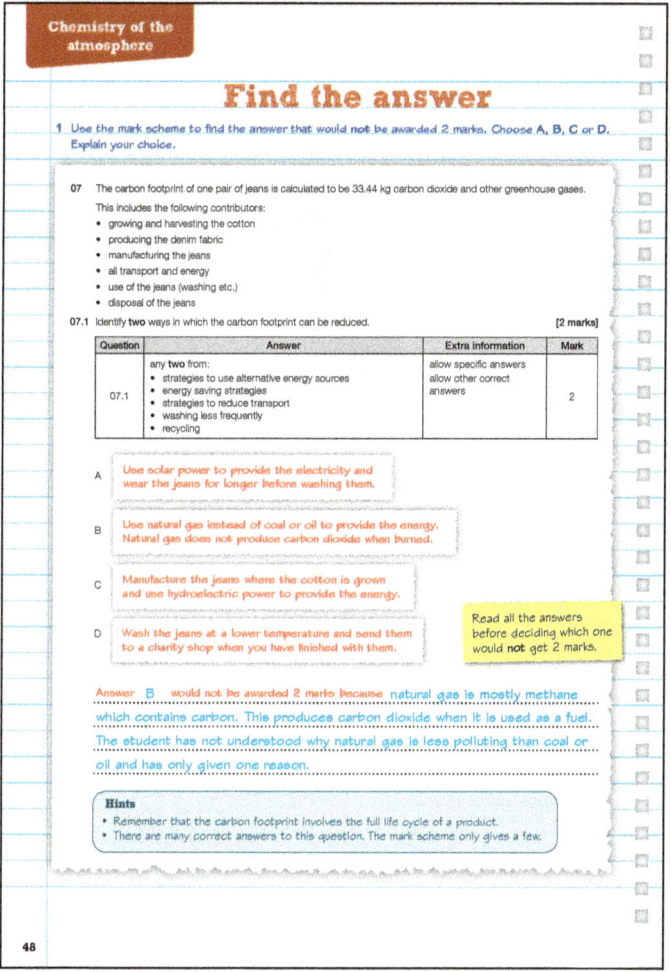

Re-order the answer

1 Rearrange the sentences below into the most logical order by numbering each part of the answer.

01 Evidence shows that the Earth is 4.6 billion years old.

There are several theories about how the Earth's atmosphere formed and has changed over time.

01.1 Describe **one** theory about how the Earth's atmosphere has changed over 4.6 billion years. **[5 marks]**

[3] The water vapour condensed to form the oceans.

[5] Plants evolved and used carbon dioxide in photosynthesis, releasing oxygen.

[1] There was intense volcanic activity during the first one billion years.

[4] Some carbon dioxide dissolved in the oceans, reducing the amount in the atmosphere.

[2] This produced an early atmosphere of mainly carbon dioxide and water vapour, with some nitrogen.

[6] The percentage of oxygen in the atmosphere allowed animals to evolve.

Think of the events as a timeline. Make the sentences tell a story.

2 Rearrange the sentences below into the most logical order by numbering each part of the answer.

01.2 Some scientists think that the evidence for the Earth's early atmosphere containing mostly carbon dioxide and water vapour is weak.

Explain why scientists might think this. **[3 marks]**

[2] Therefore ideas are often modelled on similar events that happen today.

[4] However, conditions were very different billions of years ago and this might not be true.

[1] Collecting evidence for events that happened billions of years ago is difficult.

[3] We assume the composition of volcanic gases was the same billions of years ago as it is today.

49

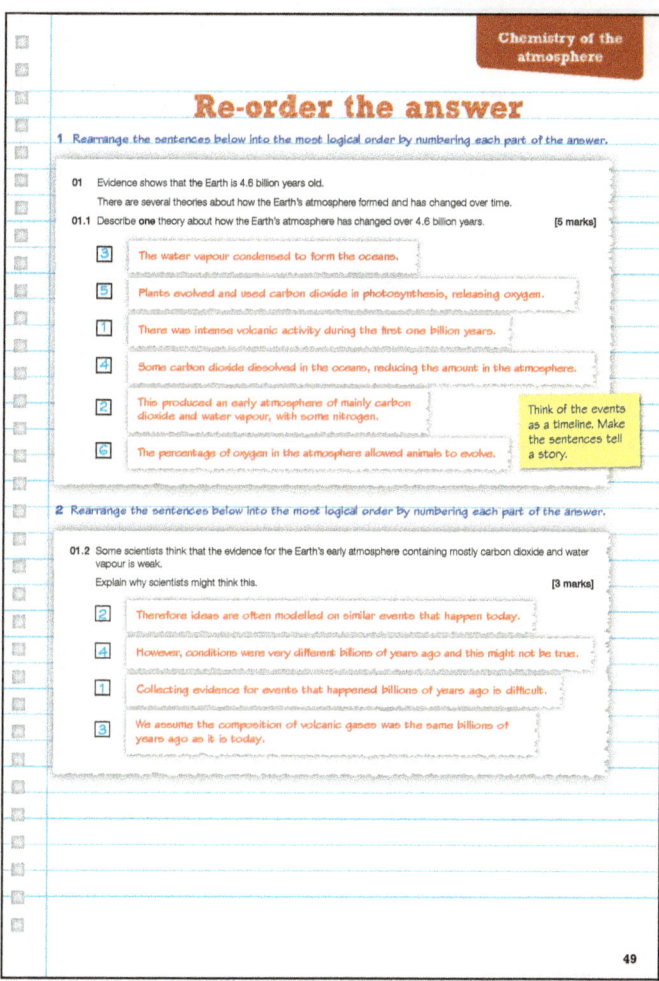

Using resources

Mark the answer

1 Draw lines to connect each of the marker's comments to the relevant part of the answer.

11 We are running out of high-grade copper ores. Areas where copper ores were once quarried still contain low-grade copper ores.

Table 10 gives some information about two methods that can be used to extract copper from low-grade ores.

Table 10

	Phytomining	Bioleaching
Method	Plants are grown in soil containing low-grade copper ore. The plants are harvested and burned. The ash contains copper compounds.	Bacteria are used to absorb copper compounds in low-grade ores. A leach solution is produced containing copper compounds.
Extracting the copper	Displacement with scrap iron or electrolysis	Displacement with scrap iron or electrolysis
Time span	A growing season	2 years

11.1 Evaluate the environmental impact of using phytomining and bioleaching to extract copper from low-grade ores. **[6 marks]**

Both methods extract the copper using scrap iron or by electrolysis, so they both need energy to do that. That usually means using fossil fuels which might run out. Growing plants on copper soils is like ordinary farming and is better to look at than mines. But the plants have to be burnt which uses electricity. Bioleaching does not need burning, but it takes a long time. The burning might give off polluting gases.

Question does not ask for comparisons with traditional mining.

Similar environmental impacts of both methods are identified.

Carbon dioxide and water given off; carbon dioxide is a greenhouse gas, but is not polluting.

A valid comparison is made.

No comparison is made.

This question continues on page 51.

'Evaluate' is a command word. You should use the information given in the question, as well as your own knowledge to consider evidence for and against.

50

Using resources

Improve the answer

1 On page 50, there is a question comparing phytomining and bioleaching. You have looked at one student's answer to this question. Write an improved answer that would be awarded 6 marks.

Suggested answer

Both methods rely on using scrap iron or electrolysis to extract the copper from the copper compounds, so the environmental impact at this stage is the same. Phytomining can be used to decontaminate ground polluted with copper ores, whereas bioleaching may add to pollution problems. Bioleaching may produce toxic chemicals which could run off into water courses and contaminate drinking water. Once it has started, bioleaching is more difficult to control in the event of a pollution problem than phytomining. Phytomining may use energy to burn the plants; bioleaching does not require energy for burning. Phytomining is limited to a growing season and needs adequate rainfall, soil nutrients and the correct temperature. Bioleaching can be carried out at any time, but takes longer than phytomining.

2 Write an improved answer that would be awarded 4 marks.

11.2 In Europe, 40% of the copper used is now produced from recycled copper.

Table 11 gives the energy requirements of each process.

Table 11

Source of copper	Energy needed to produce 1 tonne in GJ/tonne
Traditional mining	100
Recycled copper	10

Identify **two** advantages to the environment in using recycled copper rather than new copper produced by traditional mining.

Explain your answer. **[4 marks]**

Had a go

Advantage 1: Recycled copper is cheaper than new copper because it doesn't use so much energy.

Explanation: Energy is expensive.

Advantage 2: Recycled copper will not end up in landfill, but new copper might.

Explanation: We would need fewer landfill sites.

Suggested answer

Advantage 1: Less of the greenhouse gas carbon dioxide is produced from fossil fuels.

Explanation: Recycled copper requires less energy than new copper. Fossil fuels are used to provide some of our energy. These are reacted with oxygen to release energy and carbon dioxide is produced.

Advantage 2: Less agricultural land is needed for landfill sites.

Explanation: Using recycled copper rather than new copper potentially reduces the amount sent to landfill.

51

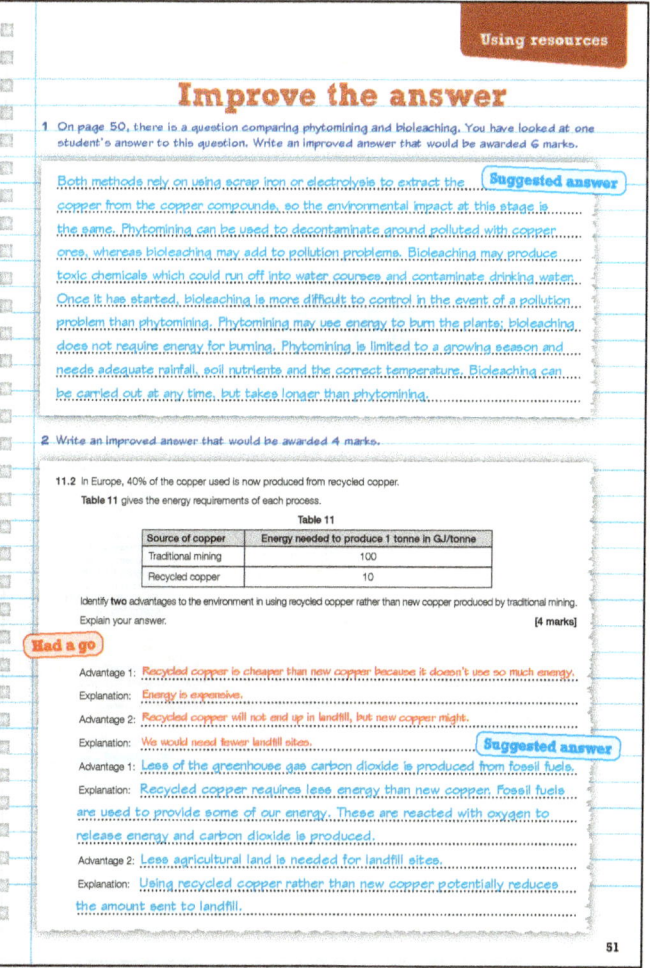

Answers

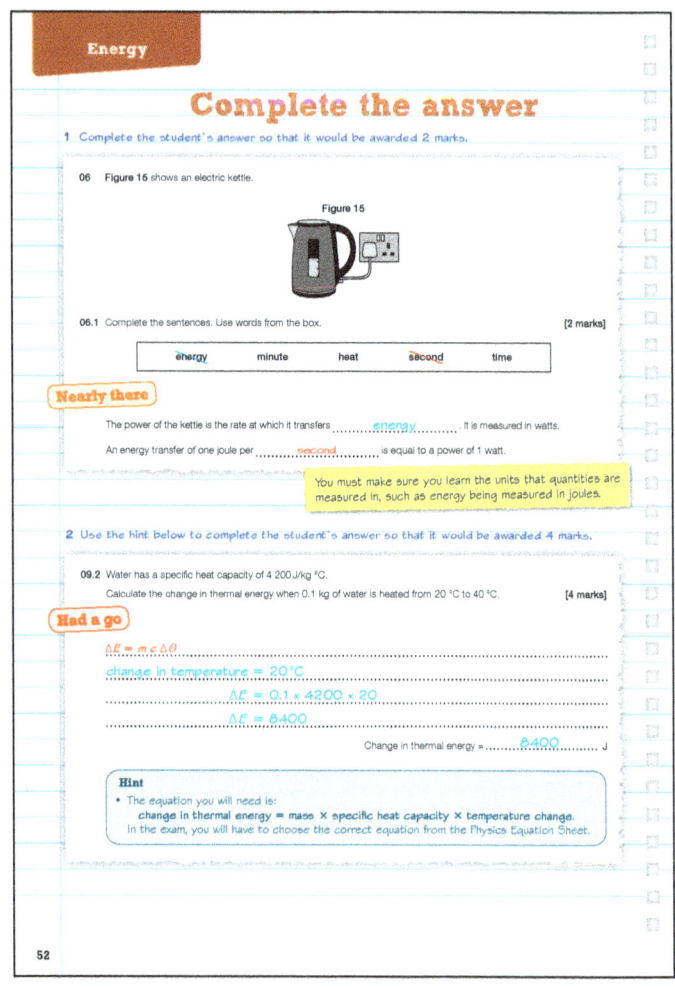

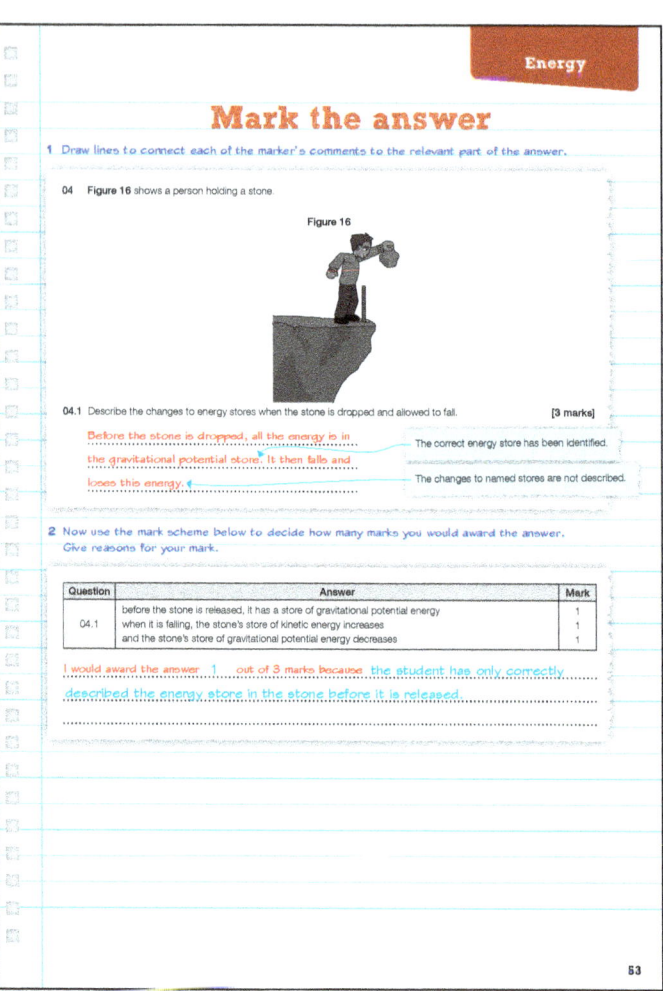

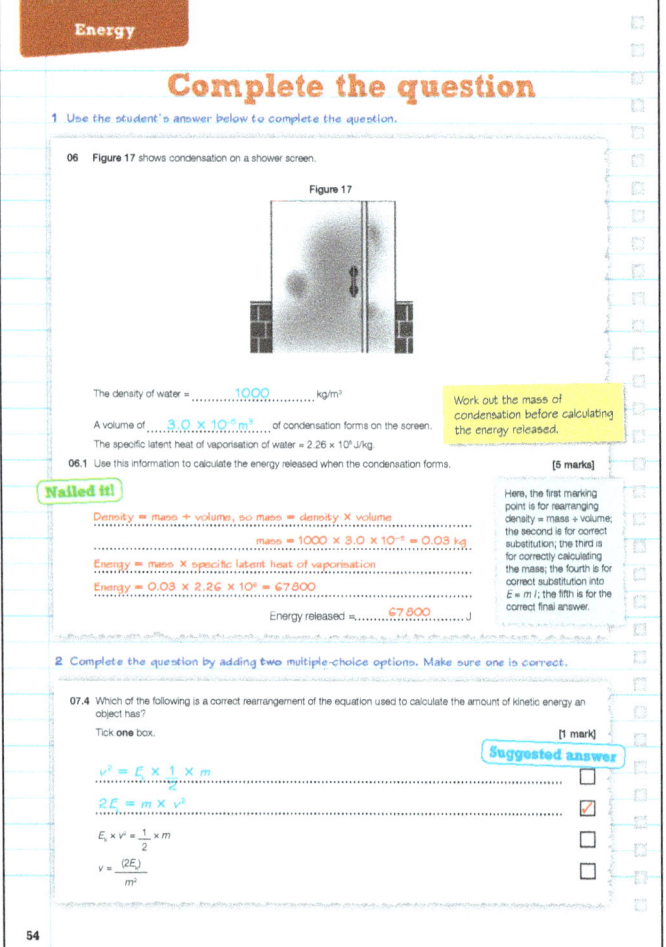

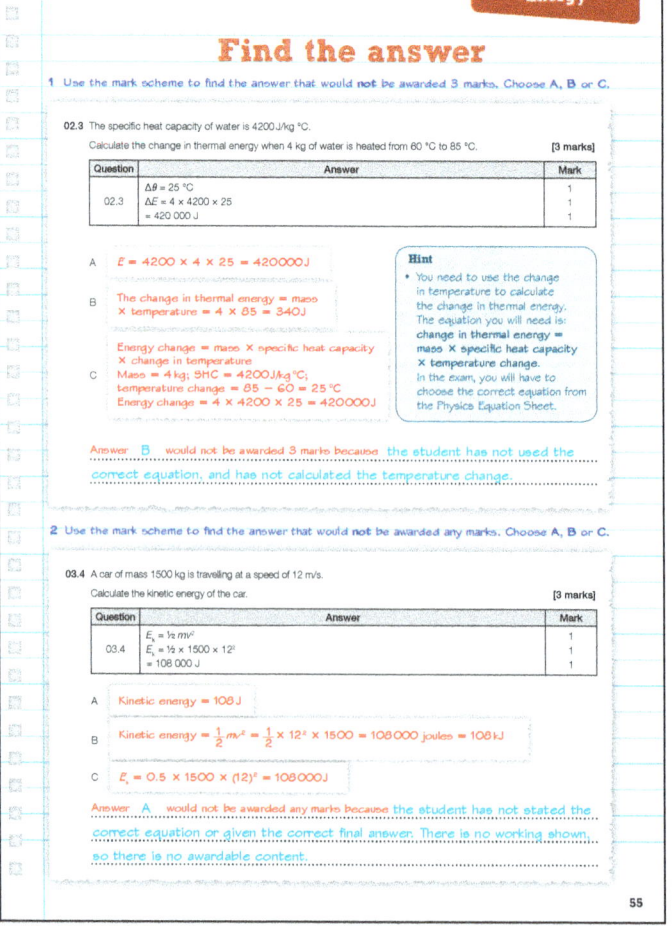

Answers

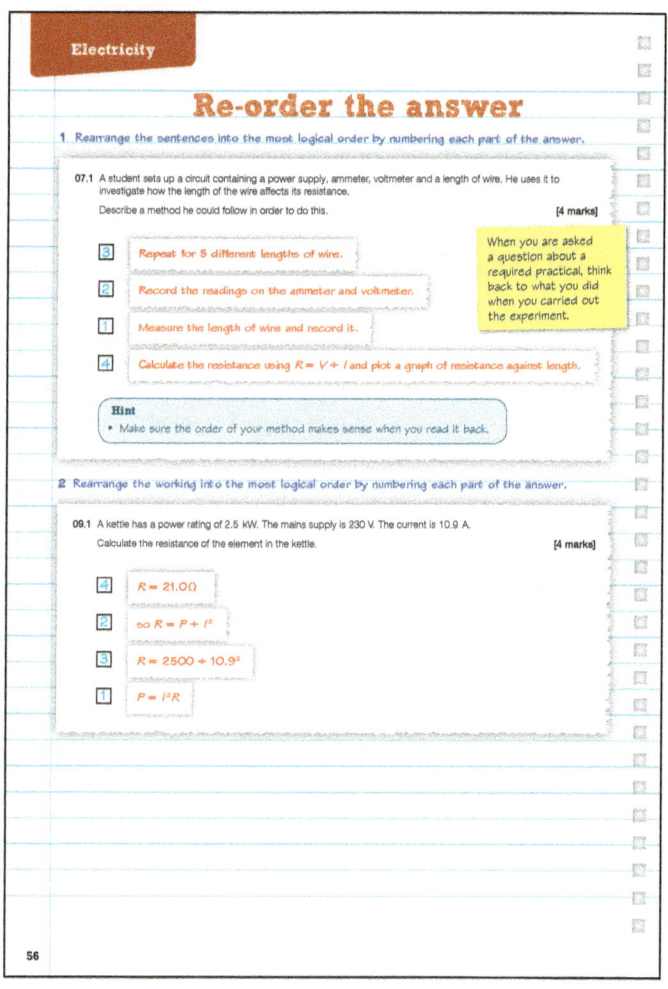

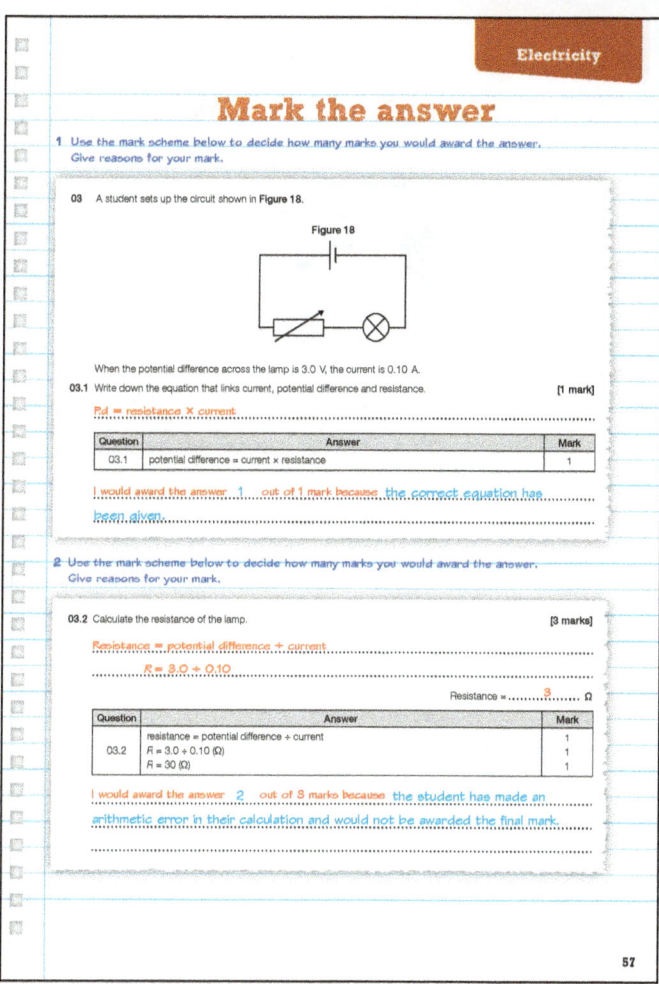

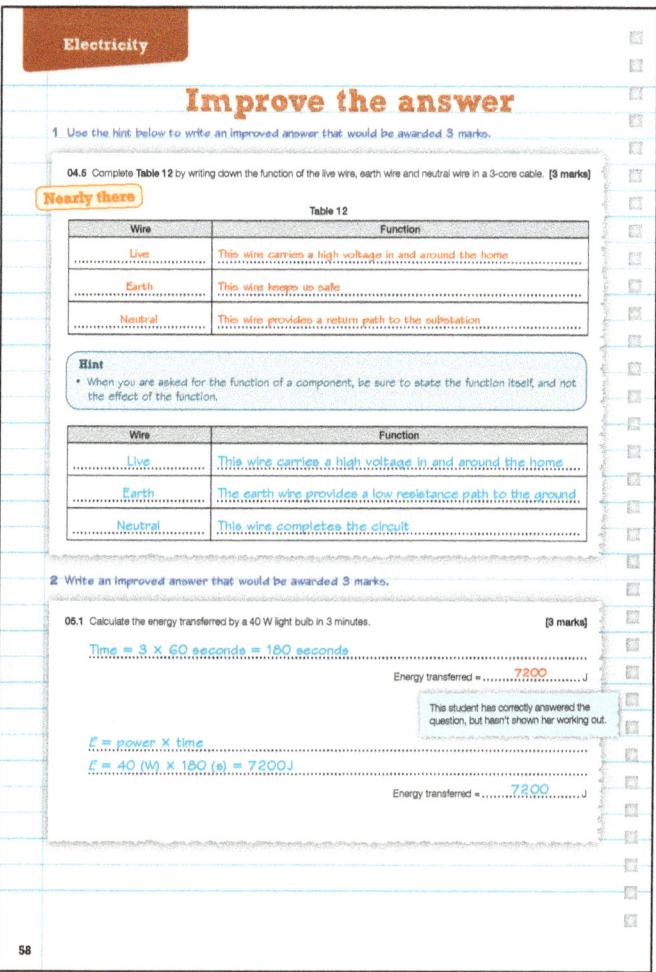

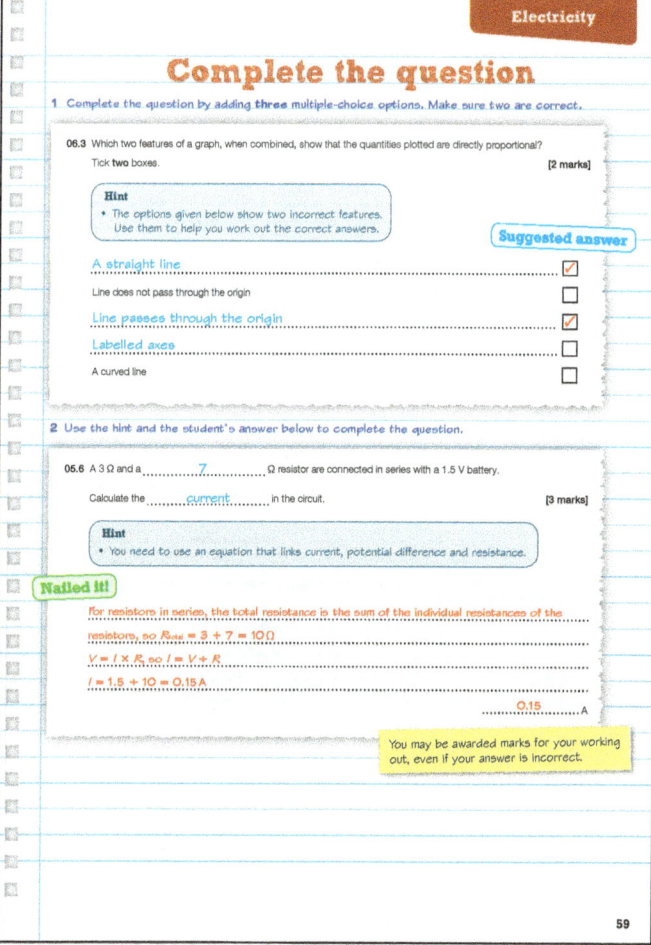

Answers

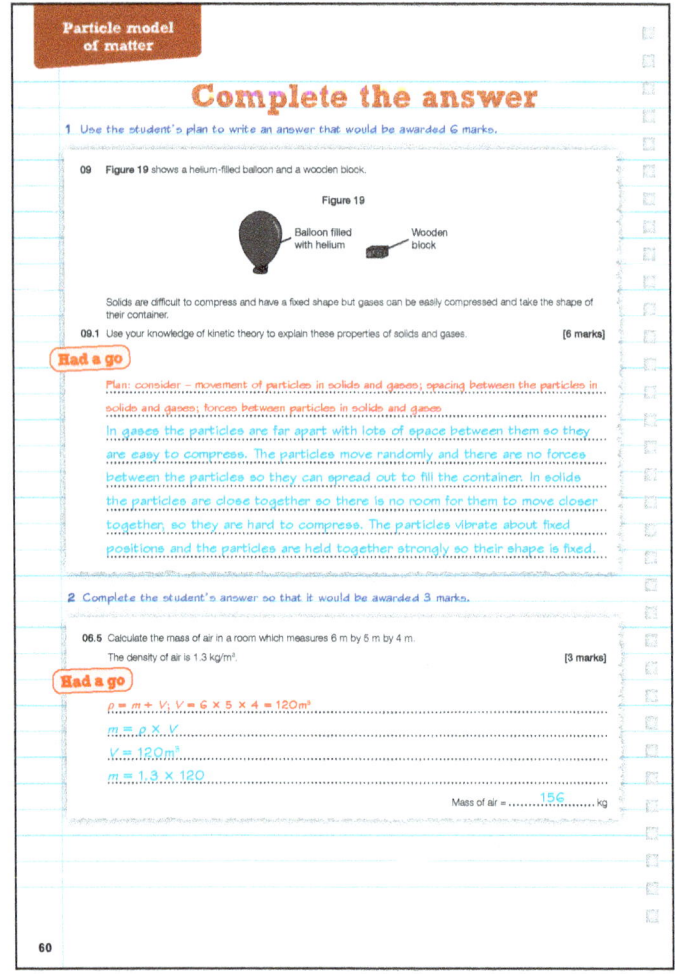

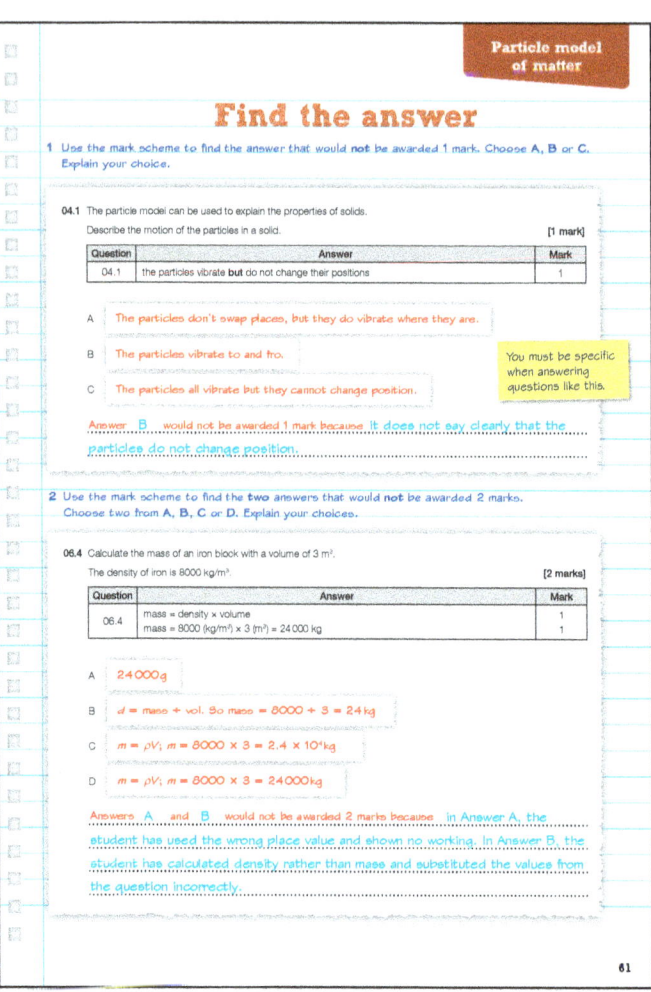

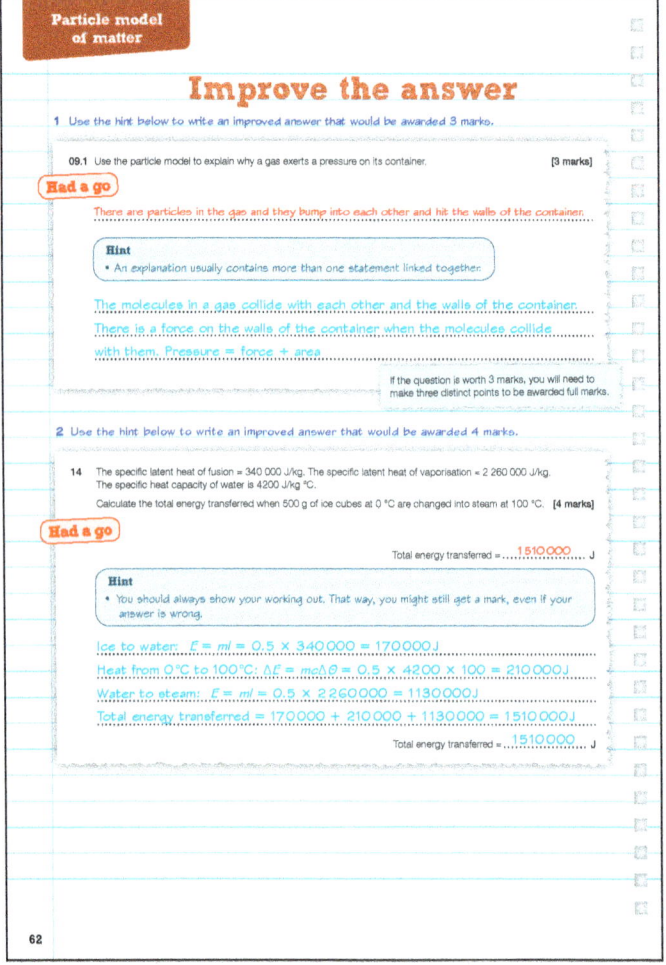

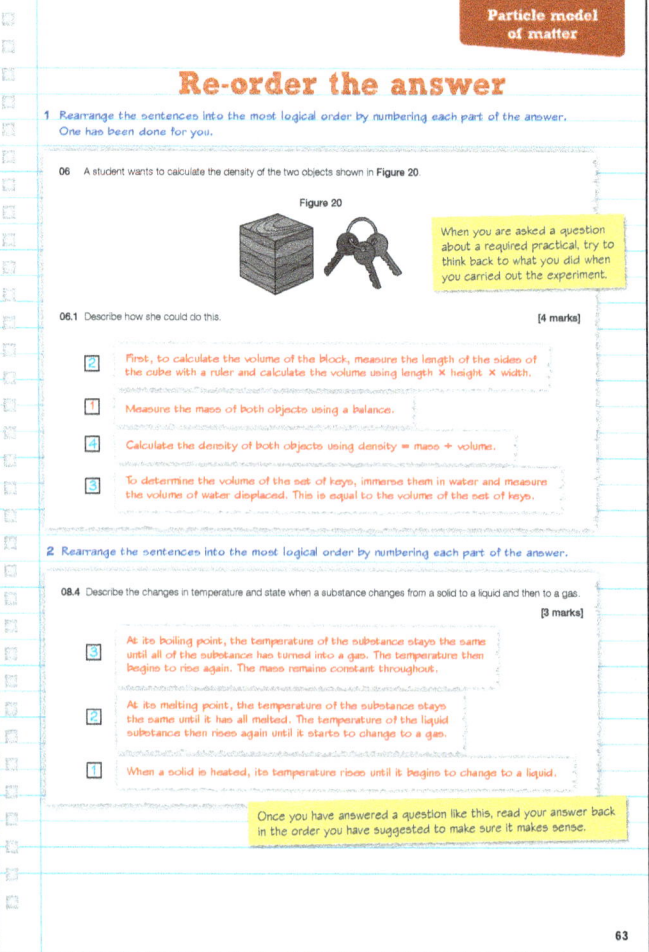

Answers

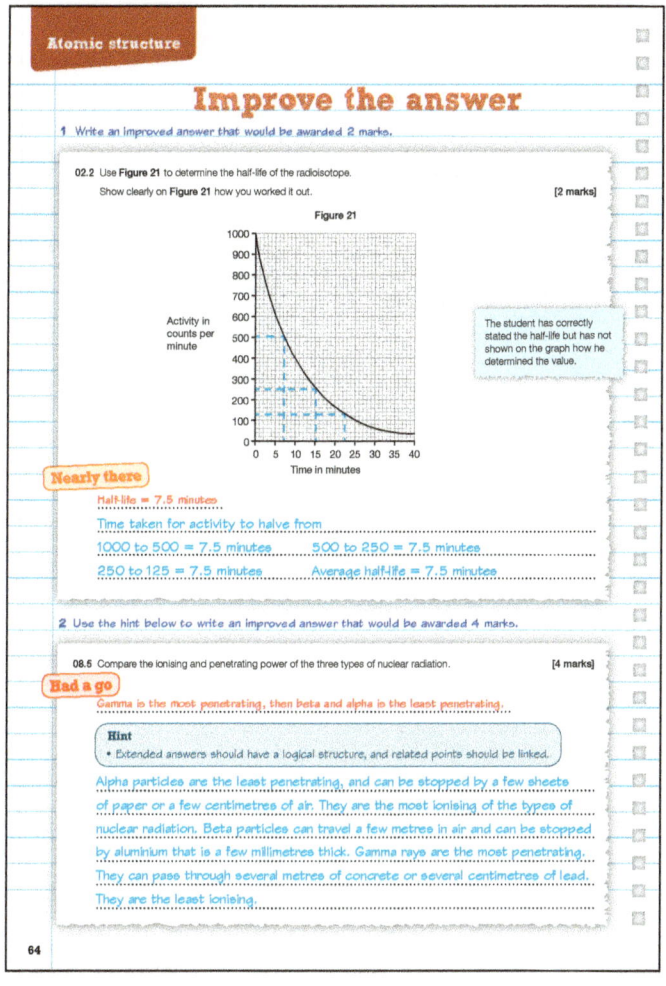

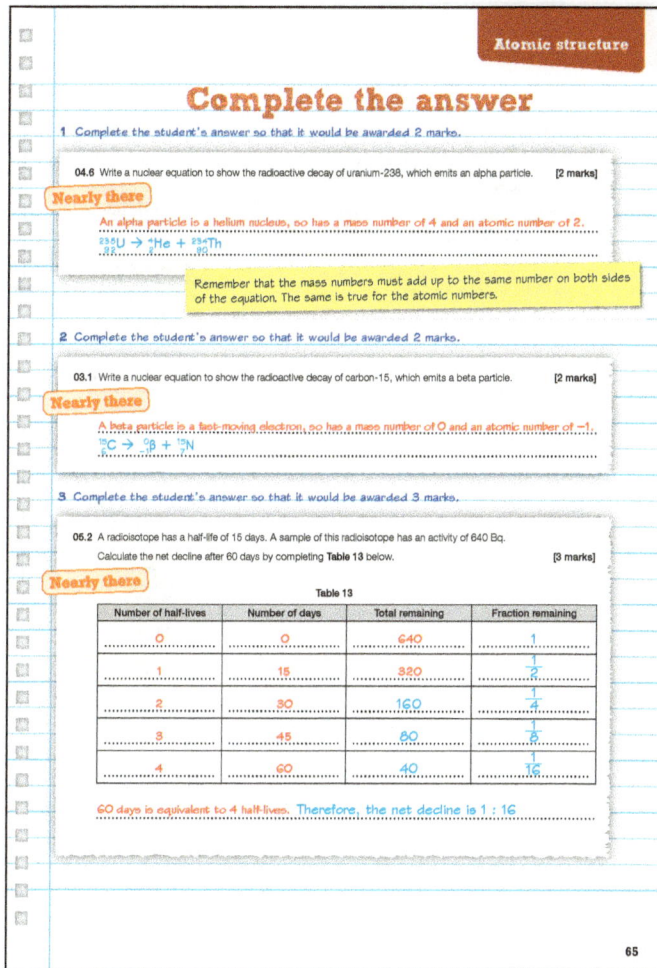

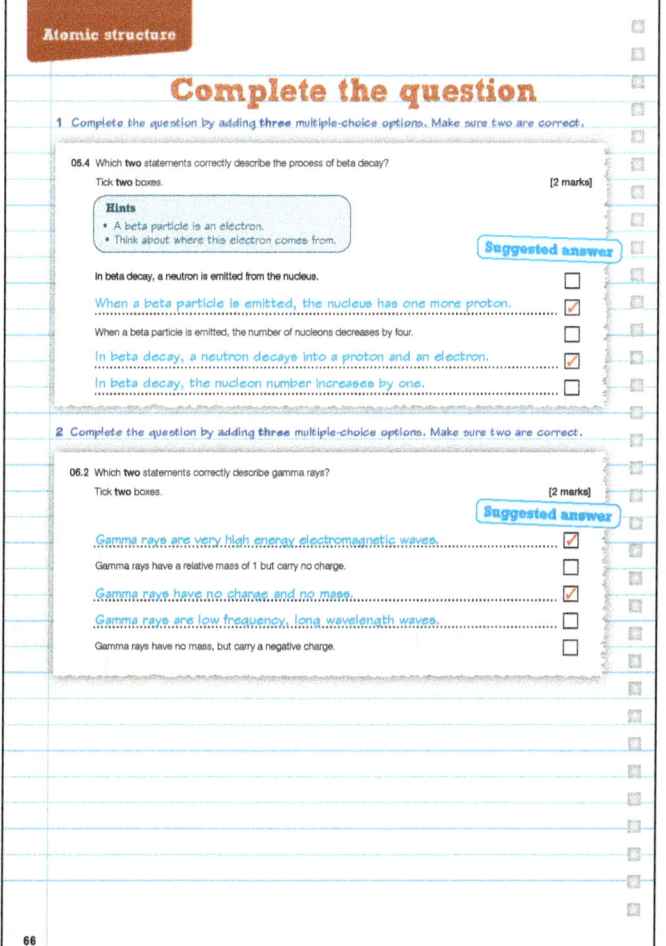

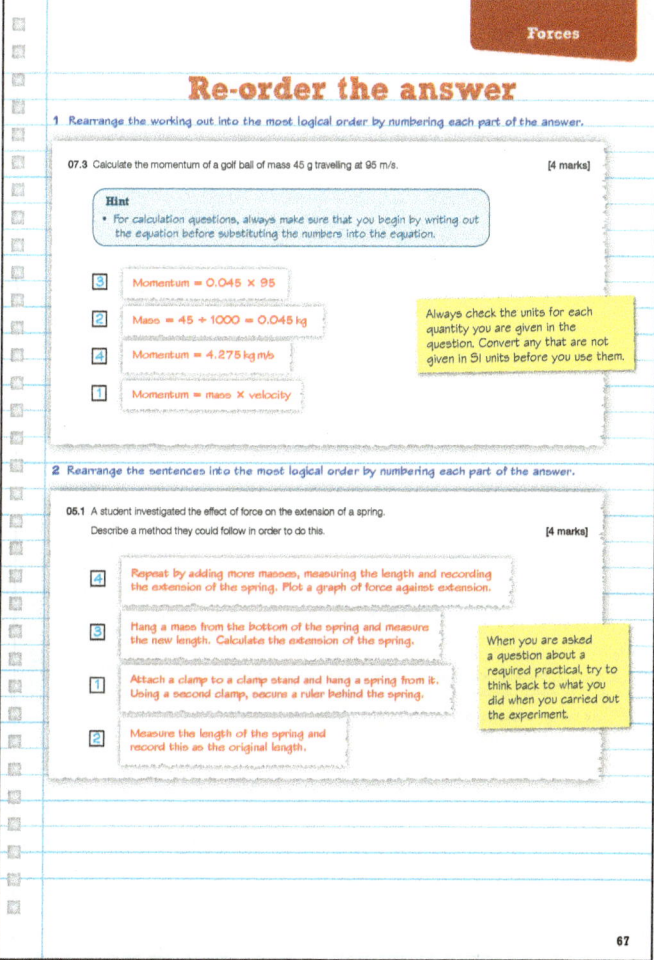

Answers

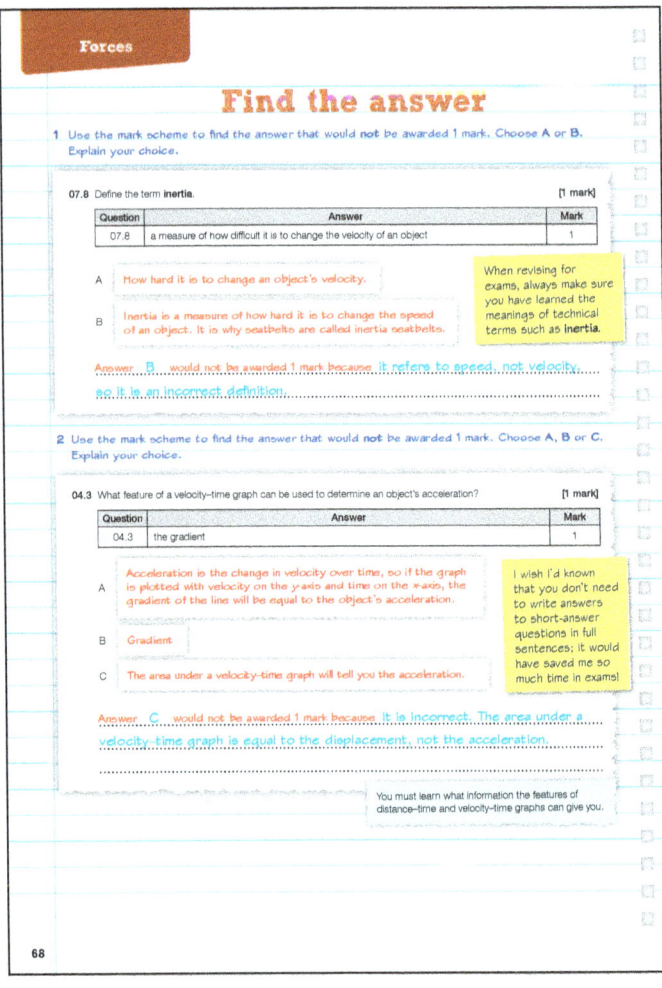

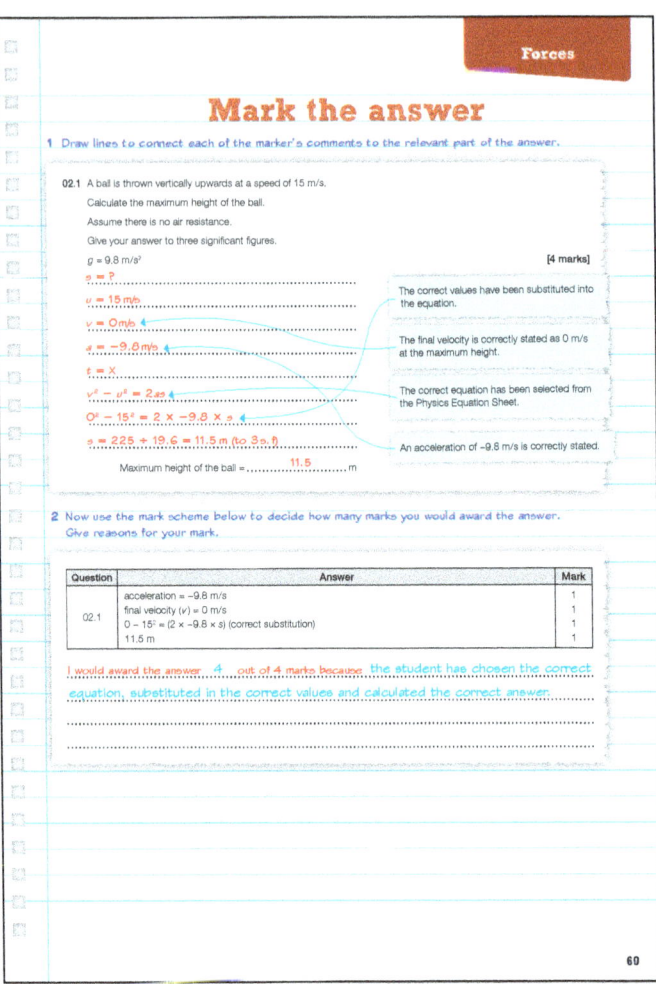

Answers

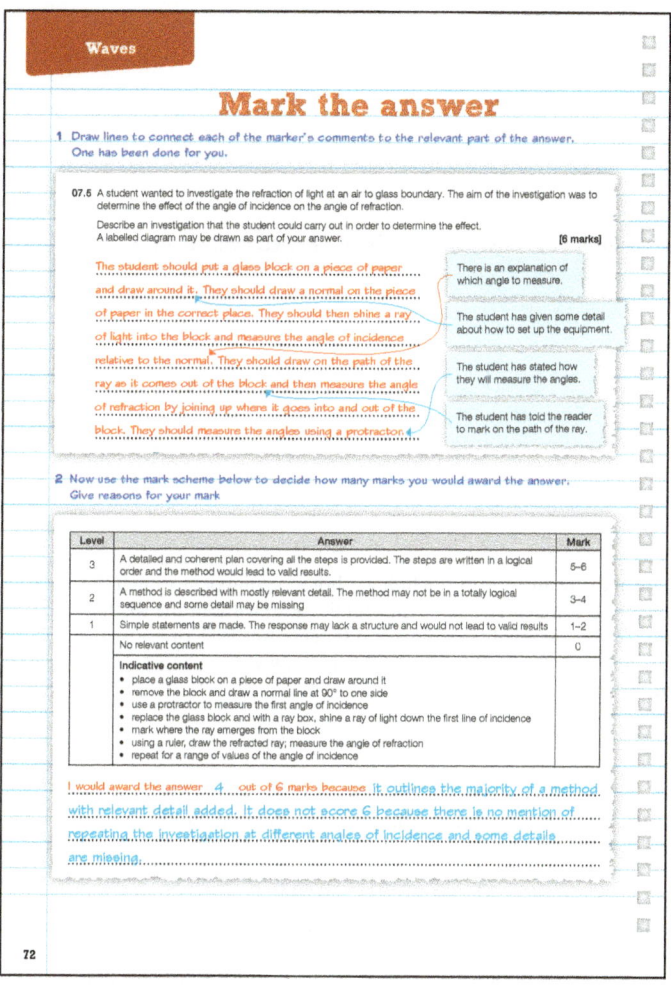

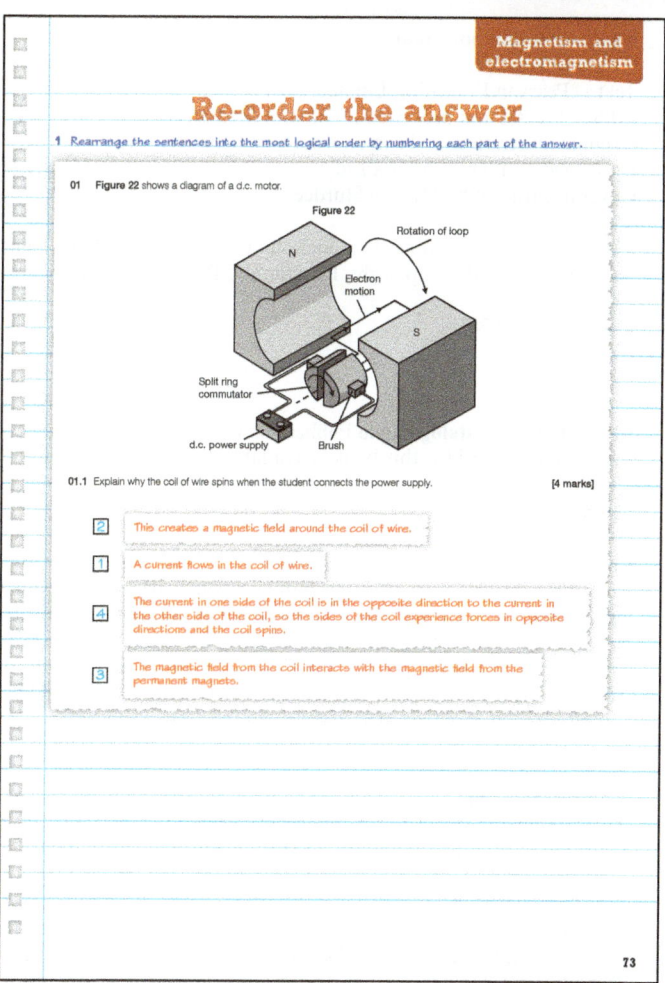

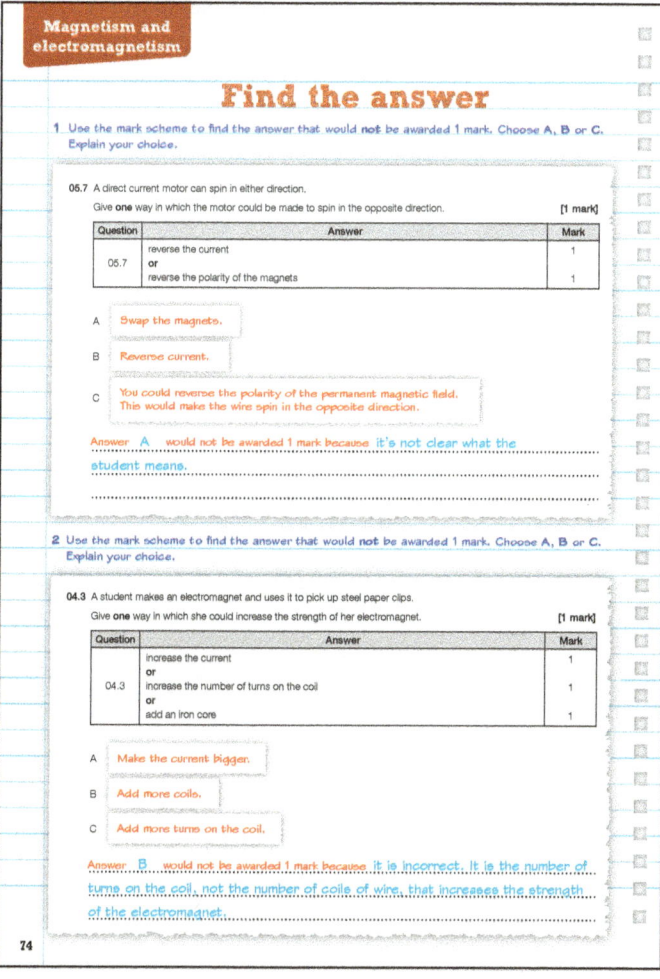

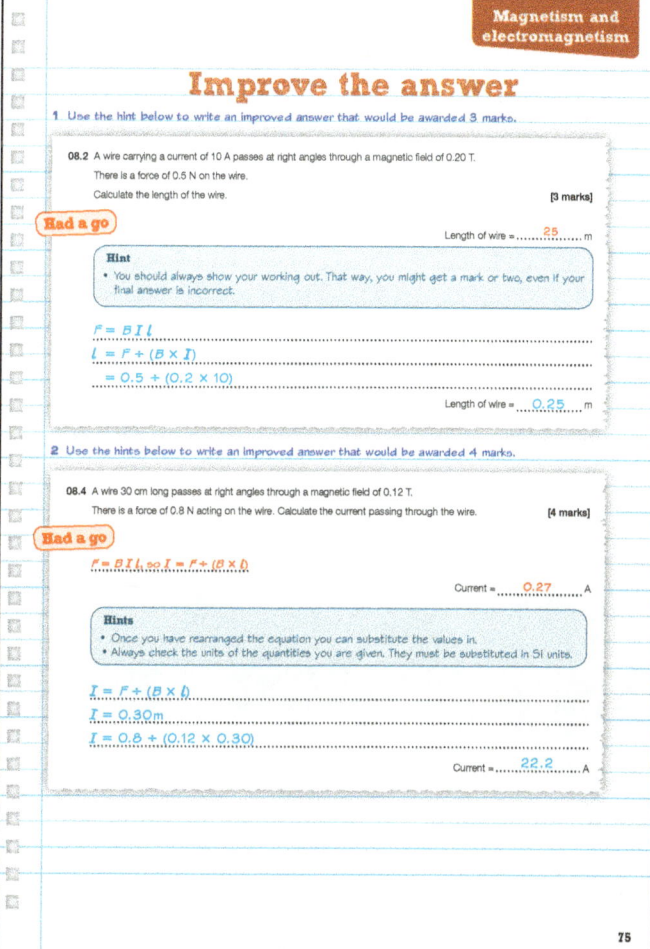

Published by Pearson Education Limited, 80 Strand, London, WC2R 0RL.

www.pearsonschools.co.uk

Text © Pearson Education Limited 2018
Edited, typeset and produced by Elektra Media Ltd
Original illustrations © Pearson Education Limited 2018
Illustrated by Elektra Media Ltd
Cover illustration by Miriam Sturdee

The rights of Anne Pilling, Lyn Nicholls and Jen Randall to be identified as authors of this work have been asserted by them in accordance with the Copyright, Designs and Patents Act 1988.

First published 2018

British Library Cataloguing in Publication Data
A catalogue record for this book is available from the British Library.

ISBN 978 1 292 23024 5

Copyright notice
All rights reserved. No part of this publication may be reproduced in any form or by any means (including photocopying or storing it in any medium by electronic means and whether or not transiently or incidentally to some other use of this publication) without the written permission of the copyright owner, except in accordance with the provisions of the Copyright, Designs and Patents Act 1988 or under the terms of a licence issued by the Copyright Licensing Agency, Barnard's Inn, 86 Fetter Lane, London, EC4A 1EN (www.cla.co.uk). Applications for the copyright owner's written permission should be addressed to the publisher.

Acknowledgements
We would like to thank Joni Sommerville, Theo Mellors, Emily Plenty, John-Paul Duddy, Emily Atkinson, Jess Salmon, Holly Coop, Matthew Foot and David Birch for their invaluable help in providing student tips for the series.

Note from publisher
Pearson has robust editorial processes, including answer and fact checks, to ensure the accuracy of the content in this publication, and every effort is made to ensure this publication is free of errors. We are, however, only human, and occasionally errors do occur. Pearson is not liable for any misunderstandings that arise as a result of errors in this publication, but it is our priority to ensure that the content is accurate. If you spot an error please do contact us at resourcescorrections@pearson.com so we can make sure it is corrected.